PRAGMATIC

PROGRAMMING

A Complete Introduction to the Pragmatic Programmer

CONNOR WALLACE

Table of Contents

Introduction 1

Chapter 1: The Aesthetics of The Source Code -
The Search for Art in Programming 11

Chapter 2: Learning A Functional Language 22

Chapter 3: Algorithms, Pseudocodes, and Structured
Programming 39

Chapter 4: The Process of Bending & Breaking 55

Chapter 5: In The Time of Coding 93

Chapter 6: Active Documentation 110

Chapter 7: Seven Problems When Testing Programs 121

Chapter 8: Quality In Software and The Continuous Integration .. 142

Chapter 9: Test-Driven Development 158

Conclusion 180

References 184

Introduction

This book "The Pragmatic Programmer" should be one of every self-respecting programmer's bedside books, and must be required reading in all computer-related courses (Computer Science, System Analysis, Data Processing, and Computer Engineering). The hype surrounding this book is justifiable because its greatest merit is shortening the gap between an inexperienced programmer and a productive and skilled professional. We will look at some concepts in this book.

The Programmer Career

We can summarize a programmer's career in the following scenario which we will later expand to with information in other chapters of this book:

- Programming logic learning and computer architecture.

- Language learning and programming techniques.

- Acting as a Junior Developer / Analyst / Consultant

- Acting as a developer / analyst / consultant

- Acting as Senior Developer / Analyst / Consultant

- Become Architect, Team Leader, Coordinator, Manager, Entrepreneur, etc.

Programmer career

Programmer programmer = new Programmer ();

programmer.learn ("Programming Logic");

programmer. learn ("Computer Architecture Basics");

programmer.learn ("language X");

while (scheduler.this Breathing () && scheduler.thisLucid ()) {

 Project project = new Project ("System | Correction | Improvement | Functionality");

// Developing

while (! project.thisReady ()) {

  if (project.isBrown ()) {

    programmer.use POG (project);

  } else {

        programmer.develop (project);

  }

  programmer.tomarCafe ();

```
}

// Maintenance

programmer.correctBugs (project);

programmer.attendCalls ();

programmer.correctNewBugs (project);

programmer.xingProgrammerWhatDoneSystem ();

// Evolution

if (developer.tiverTime ()) {

    programmer.learn (“language X”);

    programmer.learn (“API Y”);

    programmer.learning (“Z technique”);

}

// sortNumber () = random method that returns a number between 1
and 100,000,000

    if (boss.sortearNumber () == 0) {

  boss.promote (programmer);

}

}
```

The Basics

The basic prerequisite of every developer is to have good programming logic, to have at least a sense of how the computer works, and also to know a little about computer theory. So if you want to become a good trader, develop these items very well, especially logic.

This is so basic that it should not even be mentioned, but unfortunately, many programmers do not even focus on this fundamental aspect (logic), because they rush to learn how to deal with language X, IDE Y, instead of strengthening the pillar that will sustain them throughout their careers. Tip number 1 is:

- If you are starting out in the area, do not stick to IDE's, do programming in vim, notepad, or any simple text editor.

- Solve various problems of logic, data structure, algorithms, etc. There are a lot of good books on just these subjects, and in some cases, even using structured Portuguese as the language to solve them.

Those with a great programming logic base can easily learn any language, API, or framework, just as a good driver can easily learn to drive any car.

And even for experienced programmers, there's a lot to explore in the field of logic and algorithms, like:

- Complexity Analysis (notation O);
- Invariants;

- Graphs;

- Formal languages and finite automata;

- Artificial intelligence;

- etc.;

The Common Place

The next step is to learn one or more programming languages, APIs, methodologies, etc. It is the stage where most of us programmers are.

In fact, the continuous learning process is one of the hallmarks of our field and should be followed as much as possible. We must become experts in all the technologies we deal with, whether at work or home. Due to the speed with which technologies evolve and are discarded, we must always be aware of the news of the market, following specialized websites, magazines, blogs, etc. to see the directions and trends of our area.

The concept of open source is not only applicable to software but also the knowledge. We have the privilege of working at a time when diverse information on the most varied technologies is available on the internet for free.

Even with continuous learning, specialization, etc., many still feel a "vacuum" between their level of development maturity and those of the best professionals in the industry. What is the secret of these professionals to be so productive?

Pragmatism in Action

After all, what is being a Pragmatic Pro? Among all the features that the book highlights, I believe common sense stands out. But after all, how to apply common sense in our programming practice? For this, we will try to understand how this type of professional thinks.

First and foremost, a pragmatic programmer is lazy by nature and does his best to stay that way. Let's look at the main characteristics of this type of professional:

Buddhist Master

When the pragmatic programmer repeats the same task over and over, he stops and thinks, "Is there no way to automate it?" He then learns scripting languages (sed, awk, shell, etc.) or dynamic languages to automate repetitive tasks by getting rid of them. Now consider: How many repetitive tasks, whether programming-related or not, do you have in your daily routine, and how do you automate them?

- Do you analyze system log files? Create a script or program that does it for you.

- Have to submit weekly reports? Create a program that processes this.

The pragmatic programmer is like a Buddhist master, for he is always in the here and now, in the present moment, noticing what he is doing and thinking of ways to avoid repetition (after all he hates to waste time). Therefore, it seeks every kind of tool that favors task automation.

Newton's Motto

The famous physicist Isaac Newton once said, "If I saw it further than the others, it was because it was on the shoulders of giants." Pragmatic programmers fervently adopt this motto.

The pragmatic programmer does not reinvent the wheel, and he will always rely on technologies tested and approved by the software community. There are thousands of APIs and frameworks for many different purposes. The pragmatic programmer knows this and won't waste time doing something that already exists. That's why it's always up to date on existing technologies, through reading and continuous learning.

And among the solutions that exist, will always adopt, when possible, those that save typing, favor simplicity and expressiveness.

He also knows that when he comes across a programming problem, he will think that probably more people have had the same problem, and among them, someone posted the solution on the internet. Therefore, he is a frequent visitor to specialized websites, blogs, forums, and other data sources that can solve his problem quickly.

*Reflection:*And you, how much are you aware of the technologies in your area? For example, the Apache project contains dozens of frameworks for solving various everyday problems, such as Commons Lang, log4j, CLI, HttpClient, MINA Framework, etc. Have you heard of these projects? Staying informed is always being one step ahead.

Short Memory

The pragmatic programmer knows that over time he will forget how to perform routine tests on a particular module he has developed. And so you don't have to review source code, remember design decisions, or look for Excel test plans because it's lazy and doesn't like to waste energy on repetitive things, it creates unit tests for all its classes. You also know that customers will be asking for a lot of business rule changes and new features in your module, so you don't have to do regression testing manually, you implement and automate unit, functional and integration testing.

The pragmatic programmer embraces the practice of seamless integration, as it helps you automate much of the development process, such as managing system builds, running tests, monitoring system complexity, code quality level, documentation level, deploy, etc.

Reflection: How much do you know about Continuous Integration? Have you heard of Maven, Sonar, Coverage, Checkstyle, PMD, Hudson / Jenkins, Nexus, Artifactory, Mantis, Redmine, JIRA, Junit, JMock, Selenium?

Unhappy

The pragmatic programmer is a nonconformist by nature, as he is always wondering if there is a better way of doing things.

He adopts the practice of Refactoring and incremental steps because he knows he will never produce perfect first-rate software (and probably never will). You know the saying that the great is the enemy of the good. But to make continuous improvement, it is aware of the importance of supporting continuous integration and TDD to mitigate risks.

What's more, he tries to get an overview of the whole by studying how different languages and tools deal with the same problem. Seeing the problem from many different angles gives you a better view of how to solve it.

More than uncomfortable, the pragmatic programmer is clever because he doesn't want to be triggered over the weekend because the system has failed, nor have to listen to nervous bosses asking him about delivery delays or project failures. Not only does he focus on "technical" reading (because he has good logic and experience, he knows he will assimilate new technologies as he dedicates himself), but he also studies everything related to the principles of good software development practice to produce modular applications and cohesive. Know the best techniques and lean on the shoulders of giants to guide their architectural decisions.

Reflection: How much time do you devote to reading books on software quality, architecture/engineering, standards, best practices, etc.?

The pragmatic programmer does not get into "autopilot" is always thinking of new ways to do his job better by adopting concepts such as automation, continuous integration, TDD, Refactoring, modularization, standards, etc. He is, first and foremost, a thinking, critical, and responsible being who regards time as something very valuable and thus avoids waste. By adopting this process of gradual evolution, continuous improvement over one's working method, over time, one becomes an extremely productive and effective professional.

This was just a review, as the book is full of good advice on how to become a better programmer. And interestingly, there will be very little code presence in this book, and it's more like a book of philosophy, good practices, and ideas, like:

Orthogonality;

DRY - Don't Repeat Yourself;

Demeter's Law;

Refactoring;

DSL;

Tests;

etc.

So let's get started with the journey!

Chapter 1

The Aesthetics of The Source Code - The Search for Art in Programming

Acomputer language is nothing more than a set of instructions that we introduce in a machine so that it operates, allowing us to develop programs. In this way, the different ways in which we combine these instructions give rise to the different styles and schools responsible for what we can call ' the aesthetics of programming. '

That aesthetic, according to the rules to which it responds, can be classified in turn into four large groups that traditionally, like many artistic trends, have coexisted simultaneously.

The Four Aesthetics

The most anarchic group, the one where everything goes, is the one that is not defined within any school: a scramble without any order that grows organically as different needs arise. There are no deep structures or a planned arrangement; It is simply the natural result of adding more and more lines as required. We would have the first current, the organicist, vulgar, and pejoratively known as ' Spaghetti code ' for its clear tangled and complex reference. But like every organized system, programming tends to be structured coherently and logically. From this natural evolution, the rest of the lines or styles that complete the painting would emerge.

Donald Knuth identified a second order by identifying the good code with the one that he enjoys with his reading. In this way, a piece of software becomes almost a literary piece: from an initial approach or problem, we are advancing through its development in what we identify as the plot to reach the solution or outcome. Many factors are relegated to an anecdotal level under this approach since it is a composition that prevails over the rest. This current, more cultured, has historically generated as many fans as detractors.

Robert C. Martin would open a new stage by weighing the work of a programmer more statistically: according to his observations, a developer spends a tenth of his time writing code in front of nine others reading it. That disproportion motivated him to face the process from another perspective: if we spend most of our time reading it, we need to optimize that reading even if it requires more effort during its writing. Here the structural ability is no longer being valued, but the final pragmatism: beauty must not come through complex literary resources, but with the simplicity of an idea. The message of a children's story, despite its limitations, can be as beautiful as the most baroque work.

Finally, and since more recent times, a fourth current makes its way with force: that of the taste for the most refined perfectionist style. With an uncertain origin, generated perhaps spontaneously and simultaneously, this current is attributed to the academic elites of each language. They assume the swan song in terms of the possibilities offered by a system. Beauty comes here from elegance and adornment, regardless of the clarity of its final exhibition. The reader who looks at this current can be caught by perfectly designed structures, where all its elements work in a coordinated way, but whose objective is not at all clear — looking for an artistic simile.

It is not necessary to emphasize the clash between these currents: chaos against the order, and order against itself. The search for beauty from a technical approach to the simplicity with which the idea that motivates it is expressed. Finally, the most refined perfection oblivious to the pragmatism of forms. It is a debate between an endless crossfire: is complex beauty the true end of the programmer? Or maybe the goal is clarity over ornaments? What satisfies the experienced developer more? And the novel?

The Original Form: The Birth of Organic Development

As in the arts, the natural growth of a system is its first manifestation. And by natural growth, we refer to the disorganized: the first cities were constituted by accumulating homes not being until much later that they were grouped in an organized way. Much less elaborate systems preceded the neighborhoods of Tell el-Amarna or the Greek hypodermic planes.

This is, naturally, how the so-called Spaghetti Code frequently appears in the early stages of language development. A need appears, and this is solved by adding a new element to the total.

When the structures are small, this system can be maintained with some solvency. Advanced urban planning is not necessary when four neighbors found a village. Its members also do not require high technical knowledge in urban engineering and access to resources. Each inhabitant, like each small code fragment, is more or less independent of the rest. They may be needed in certain circumstances, but that does not make it necessary to have an entire Social Administration system.

However, as the community grows, the needs of organized systems arise naturally. It is still possible to maintain the old order, but as relations become more complex, so is communication and access to resources. With the code, the same thing happens: as parts are assembled, the interconnections require a formal structure, a system on which to develop logically.

At a critical point, the organic becomes ineffective and unsustainable. The effort to work without a structure demands great efforts, and with each new need, new problems arise. Just like the old Arab suburbs showed their shortcomings in the past, an old unstructured program is presented as a serious problem when it comes to working.

But as we have agreed above, that need for an organization found solutions early: if a grid was soon superimposed on the city, similar modules were also applied to the source code.

The Structure as a Basic Organization

Even when a system is structured, it does not have to be beautiful. If we turn to the old Greek cities, we will remember there the greatness of its temples and civic spaces, its gardens, sculptures, and monuments; a whole series of ornaments that respected the organizational system - the module - and that broke the monotony of other vacuums devoid of appeal. Consequently, large urban projects based exclusively on modulation have proven to be practically uninhabitable because they suffer from this care for aesthetics despite their perfect mathematical disposition.

The source code again reflects this reality: the structure, the organization, and its modularity do not make it aesthetically beautiful by itself. He needs that something else; demand that attention for the forms that the Arts proudly exhibit. As with a written text, not only does it matter what is being transmitted, but interest is given to how this is achieved.

The Aesthetics of The Code is Born

A tool that is born with purely practical objectives may unexpectedly become a work of art. Possibly, the original purpose of armor was to offer protection in combat against enemy packaging, but that does not prevent them from being used as a symbol of power in the sixteenth century to the detriment of their original purpose.

Just as the Etruscan goldsmiths demonstrated their expertise by preparing the most beautiful watermarks for their votive jewels, the current Swiss watchmaker wants to demonstrate that they are still leading this art by including more complications in their most exclusive models. Thus, whatever the ultimate goal, both perspectives seek distinction through the relationship of aesthetics and technique.

Within that scheme of thought is where the philosophy of Donald Knuth fits. For this pioneer in Computer Science, mathematician, and an emeritus professor at the prestigious Stanford University, the code must be organized as the most elaborate literary pieces do. In his great work, The Art of Computer Programming, he defends all these ideas.

> *We have seen that computer programming is an art since it applies accumulated knowledge to the world, because it requires skill and ingenuity, and especially because it can produce objects of great beauty.*

> *A programmer who subconsciously sees himself as an artist will enjoy what he does and will do better.*

> *- Donald Knuth, acceptance speech for the Turing Award (1974)*

For the mathematician, 'instead of providing a machine with instructions with what we want to do, we must concentrate on explaining to others what we want the machine to do. ' Now, the ultimate goal of a program does not rest on the computer that interprets it, but on the programmers who make it. The structure of the software must be structured according to the human being; the source code is the logical illustration of what is exposed.

Art Becomes Practical With the Aesthetics of The Message

If Knuth represents the most perfectionist path by putting aesthetics before pragmatism, Robert C. Martin, familiarly known as Uncle Bob (Uncle Bob), sacrifices the precision of the forms to underline the importance of the final result. We are not talking about a radical break here, but about an evolution towards another more sustainable stage.

Crossed out by critics as a step back when it comes to forms, art emerges from its ornaments: from the technical demand and the motley visual display of an overwhelming Baroque, we turn to the robustness of the Rationalism of the 20th century where the end prevails over the form. The perfectly calculated structure persists but remains hidden; It is not displayed excessively: unjustified excesses do not like, they are taken as a distraction that takes the viewer away from the message.

For Martin, the code, like Art, must be structured so that it complies with a series of basic principles. Namely:

- Be simple - not simple - expressive, and readable.

- Respond to a single well-defined purpose.

- Use the minimum necessary means without resorting to duplicity or repetition.

While the expressiveness and readability inherited from Knuth's approach are necessary, we now seek simplicity and minimalism. The code must be the tool that solves one - and only one - need, being a program of an ordered sequence of said fragments, unique and well defined.

Returning to our literary similes, the author of a work must review each written paragraph at its end, checking whether some reiterations or figures do not enrich the set. The creative process is complemented by an arduous task of sanitation and simplification, provided that the initial idea remains unchanged. Work will be better valued if still maintaining the message and the original expressiveness, and it is brief.

The Code Today - Extreme Refining and Precision as The Main Objective

Finally, we reach the realm of the most excellent expertise. The creators have a whole tradition behind them that serves as a starting point for their research and complex experiments.

Again the 20th century gives us in Art the most exuberant examples of the hand of modernism, High Tech, or deconstructivism, to name just a few examples. Just look at the premises of the latter to immediately transfer it to the source code:

> *Deconstructivism is a movement characterized by fragmentation, the non-linear design process, interest in the manipulation of ideas on the surface of structures, and apparently, non-Euclidean geometry. These ideas are used to distort and dislocate some of the elementary principles of architecture, such as the structure and envelope of the building. The final visual appearance of the deconstructivist school works is characterized by stimulating unpredictability and controlled chaos.*
>
> *- Deconstructivism. Wikipedia, The Free Encyclopedia.*

The works of this stage thus stand out for an unparalleled technical perfection: the complex calculation to which each of its elements is subjected constitutes a true manifesto about the excellence of its architects. It is not surprising, therefore, that only the best in each art adhere to this trend, seeking to recognize their peers.

When we move this scenario to the field of computing, we observe that indeed this current exists and is, in addition, gaining strength. Always promoted from large companies with their best experts at the helm, they show how far the limits of each of the languages worked are mastered. A display of technical knowledge that they have transformed into a new art: codes are fragmented into interdependent modules that act as black boxes, linearity is broken, looking for the cyclomatic optimization of their algorithms through parallel systems.

Thus, the result is a product of almost unpredictable functionality at first but perfectly calculated and balanced. The developer who faces these pieces finds a priori baffling structures that end up running accurately and efficiently. The message is completely lost, diluted between technical resources and complex formulas much more inaccessible than what has preceded it.

We do not speak here of the hidden keys of art apprehendable only to the initiated, but to true mental challenges. It is recurrent that in the face of these demonstrations, the rest of the professionals will not be able to assess what is really more surprising: that the code works or the path traveled until it is reached.

On this occasion, the clash with the previous schools is insurmountable. We are not facing a natural evolution, as was the case with the forms of an idea, but with a new system that requires a different approach. The aesthetic remains, even with much more force due to the fascination it awakens, but the pragmatism has completely disappeared. You speak only to the machine, in your own language, not to humans: any logical shortcut that supposes a computational advantage will be incorporated immediately even if that means a new puzzle in the eyes of the reviewer.

As you would expect, if a traditional architect is clearly overwhelmed when facing reform in the architecture of these characteristics, the average programmer cannot participate in a language that he can hardly read in order. However, that does not deprive that, just as the roughest bricklayer can delight in solutions that he does not quite understand, the developer can recognize the elegance of what is completely out of reach. We moved here in the world of complex aesthetics.

It remains to be commented that this high qualification profile does not have to be synonymous with pedantry, although we cannot affirm that it is free of it. The most perfectionist researcher can always be willing to share his knowledge, explaining his solutions in detail to bring them closer to those interested. In this case, the technical level of his work may be due more to a natural result of his experience than to the mere demonstration of his abilities. However, there is also the opposite extreme: one who strives to obfuscate his work through the most convoluted solutions voluntarily. In this case, what he shows in his work is completely artificial and intentional, a firm demonstration of muscle: the better, the more it intimidates.

The Real World

Is there then a correct posture? Should a current prevail over the rest?

In Art, there is no answer. There will be those who like rhetoric and forms thus advocating the most cultured current; others will be more attracted to simplicity and minimalism thereby adhering to the pragmatic line; Finally, the most advanced theorists and researchers will enjoy the challenge of creating more and more complex solutions that demonstrate all that effort used during the search for their limits. Of course, those who, either due to ignorance or due to lack of means, prefer freedom over bohemian acting outside of every school and system.

In the Art of Programming, the parallelism remains identical: all aesthetics have a place simultaneously, justified, or not by their own context. And it is up to each of us to take sides during the development of our professional activity.

Chapter 2

Learning A Functional Language

Functional languages are a family of languages that most programmers have heard of, but unfortunately, not many know them well enough. And I say "unfortunately" because, even though for one reason or another functional language is in very little demand in the labor market, learning them can provide us with many interesting ideas, patterns, good habits, and lessons that we can apply to many other languages.

It is difficult to draw a clear line between functional and non-functional languages, but we can cite Lisp, Haskell, Erlang, Scala, and Clojure as the most popular functional languages today. Many popular programming languages have some functional features, such as JavaScript, Ruby, and Python. Functional languages, or in general, any paradigm to which we are not accustomed, can give us ideas that we can apply not only in these languages that have functional features but in almost any language.

Learning a functional language well enough to get some ideas and inspiration doesn't have to take long. Also, we have not only the

Internet but also excellent books that are designed precisely for programmers who come from other languages. The rest of this chapter explores some techniques, good habits, and common ideas in functional languages, which we can easily apply in other languages. Of course, some of these lessons can be learned simply by experience, and are not necessarily exclusive to functional languages.

Languages Are Different

Programming languages are like human languages in many ways: they have common syntax, common expressions, they are better or worse than others at expressing certain ideas, they can be "spoken" more or less fluently, and it can even be said that their "speakers" have a certain "culture" that is different from the "speakers" of other languages.

Thus, when we learn a new language, it is a mistake to see it as "a new syntax": learning a language well, makes us change how we think and how we solve problems. For example, let's say we start learning Lisp, and we only know "classic" imperative languages like C or Java. As part of a program we are writing, we have a function that calculates the total value to be paid for some items. The input parameters are the amount of each item, the number of items, the percentage of tax, and the limit beyond which the tax must be applied (e.g., we have two items at 5 euros each, a tax of 10 % and a limit of 8 euros; the final price will be 11.) One way to write it in Lisp would be as follows:

```lisp
(defun calculate-price-BAD (cost nitems limit percent-tax)
  (setq total-price (* cost nitems))
  (if (> total-price limit)
      (progn
        (setq tax (* total-price (/ percent-tax 100)))
        (setq total-price (+ total-price tax))))
  total-price)
```

A bad example of how to solve it in Lisp (calculate-prices-bad.lisp)

However, if we write the function this way, we don't learn anything new, and we show our "foreign accent" when writing Lisp. This code is not readable by either Java or Lisp programmers, and we don't take advantage of the language's advantages while suffering its disadvantages. We just use Lisp as "bad Java." Compare the previous code with the following one:

```lisp
(defun calculate-price (cost nitems limit percent-tax)
  (let* ((total-price (* cost nitems))
         (tax         (* total-price (/ percent-tax 100))))
    (if (> total-price limit)
        (+ total-price tax)
      total-price)))
```

Solution using Lisp more conventionally (calculate-prices.lisp)

This code is more like what many Lisp programmers would expect or write themselves, and most people who know a little about Lisp will find it more readable and easier to maintain. The reason is that we are playing to Lisp's strengths, rather than trying to adapt the language to our previous knowledge.

Specifically, the second example takes advantage of two very common details in Lisp that are not so common in non-functional languages:

- Do not use variables, but "named values." Or, in other words, avoid assigning more than once to each variable. This can be seen in the let block*: the two "variables" in the block, total-price, and tax, never receive other values. Thus, the let block* contains a list of values with symbolic names, which makes the code clearer and more maintainable.

- The if-construction follows the functional pattern of being an expression that returns a value. In this case, it receives a condition and two expressions: the first is returned if the condition is true, and the second if the condition turns out to be false. It works in a similar way to the ternary operator of C and Java (value = condition ? truevalues : falsevalues).

Knowing this, and that the last expression of a Lisp function is the value returned by it, the second example can be understood much better.

Thinking About The Goal, Not The Process

Although the above example is quite simplistic, it also illustrates that functional languages tend to make you think more about the goal than the process. For algorithms, generally, a solution in a functional language is more like a mathematical definition. In the first example, the implementation of the function is based on the process of calculation. In the second, in the meaning of operations. If we think about it, the first example would be something like this:

First, we multiply the cost by nitems to calculate the base price and save it in total-price. If it is above the limit, then we first calculate tax by multiplying total-price by percent-tax divided by 100, and then we save in total-price the sum of the old total-price plus tax. The result is the total-price saved value at the end of the process.

The second example, however, would be something like this:

The result is the sum of total-price and tax if total-price is above the limit, or total-price otherwise. We define total-price as the multiplication of cost by nitems, and tax as the multiplication of total-price by percent-tax divided by 100.

Note how in the second explanation, we can leave for the end the explanation of the values declared in the let block*. In many cases, and as long as we have chosen good names for those values, it will not be necessary to read the let* block to understand the function.

Using variables that do not change once we have assigned them a value is a good habit because it makes it easier to understand where each value comes from. For that reason, the Scala language distinguishes between two types of variables: var and val. The second type, which is by far the most used, declares an immutable variable, so the compiler assures us that we cannot assign any other value once it has been declared.

This is related to the following section, "Bottom-up design, small functions": to think about the meaning, many of the operations have to be abstracted into small functions.

Bottom-Up Design, Small Functions

Another common feature of Lisp programming is to try to bring the language closer to the task at hand. One of the ways to do this is to write functions that, although small and simple, hide implementation details that do not interest us and that raise the level of abstraction. The lesson here is that writing one- or two-line functions and methods are useful if they raise the level of abstraction. It's not about "hiding code" so as not to have it in sight, and it's about making you forget part of the complexity of the task you are performing.

As an example, let's continue with the previous case of prices and items. One of the operations we do is to calculate a certain percentage. If we assume that it is an operation that we will use more than once, it might make sense to abstract that calculation. We are not going to save lines of code, but this version may require less mental effort and be easier to read (imagine the following example, as we did in the previous section):

```
In the case of Lisp, we could have called this function '%', so
The call below would be '(% percent-tax total-price)' (defun
percentage (percent amount)
  (* amount (/ percent 100)))

(defun calculate-price (cost nitems limit percent-tax)
  (let* ((total-price (* cost nitems))
         (tax          (percentage percent-tax total-price))
    (if (> total-price limit)
      (+ total-price tax)
      total-price)
```

Solution by abstracting the calculation of percentages (calculate-prices.lisp)

Calculating a certain percentage is trivial, and by writing the function percentage, we are not saving lines of code, but every second we save in understanding trivialities by reading the source is one more second that we can dedicate to more important matters. And the time we need to understand code without the appropriate abstractions often grows exponentially, non-linearly, as new abstractions are added.

Another advantage of abstracting functions in this way is that these functions are usually quite easy to test because they tend to have simple interfaces and clear responsibilities. In the case of languages that have an interactive console (such as Lisp, Python, Ruby, and others), it is easy to experiment with the function and see what it does, facilitating the writing of unit tests in any language. Especially if we avoid the side effects, as we will see in the next section.

Side Effects

So-called side effects are one of the most important concepts in functional programming, if not the most important. This is what differentiates purely functional languages from non-pure functional languages. Even programmers of languages that are not purely functional (such as Lisp) generally try to avoid side effects.

A side effect is any change that a function produces outside the scope of the function itself. For example, a function that changes a variable it has received as a parameter (i.e., "input/output parameters") or that changes global variables or anything other than local variables to the function is producing side effects. This includes any input/output, such as reading or writing files or interacting with the screen, keyboard, or mouse.

Why is it so important to avoid side effects? Again, as with small functions that raise the level of abstraction, avoiding a single side effect is not a very big advantage. However, avoiding side effects as a general rule makes programs easier to understand and maintain, and there are fewer surprises. The reason is that avoiding side effects ensures that no error in function can affect anything else.

If we also do not refer to anything external to the function, such as global variables, we have a very important extra guarantee: the function is independent from the rest of the code, which means that no failure in the rest of the program can affect our function and that we can test the function independently from the rest of the code, which is not only practical but makes it easier to make sure that we cover all possible cases of the function with test batteries.

Let's look at an example of side effects in Python. The sort method, unfortunately, changes the list it is called. This can lead to unpleasant surprises, as we will see in the first example. Let's say we're writing a program to manage racing competitions and we write a function best_time that receives a list of numbers and returns the least (we obviate the existence of the min function to make the example more illustrative):

```python
def best_time_BAD(list):
  if len(list) == 0:
    return None
  list.sort()
  return list[0]

times = [5, 9, 4, 6, 10, 8]
best_time_BAD(times)   # Return 4
print times            # This prints "[4, 5, 6, 8, 9, 10]"!
```

Unpleasant surprise due to a side effect (best-time-bad.py)

One way to solve this problem is to use the sorted function instead of the sort method:

```python
def best_time(list):
  if len(list) == 0:
    return None
  return sorted(list)[0]

times = [5, 9, 4, 6, 10, 8]
best_time(times)   # Return 4
print times        # Print "[5, 9, 4, 6, 10, 8]"
```

Better implementation, no side effects (best-time-bad.py)

Ruby usually uses the convention of adding a "!" to the end of the method name if it produces side effects (another convention you can see in the example is how methods that return true/false end in "?"). The example above could be translated to Ruby as follows:

```ruby
requires                  # Pretty printer

def best_time_BAD(list)
  if list.empty?
    nil
  else
    list.sort!            # "sort!", with side effects!
    list[0]
  end

times = [5, 9, 4, 6, 10, 8]
best_time_BAD(times)   # Return 4
pp times               # Print "[4, 5, 6, 8, 9, 10]"


def best_time(list)
  if list.empty?
    nil
  else
    list.sort[0]         # "sort", without
  end
end

times2 = [5, 9, 4, 6, 10, 8]
best_time(times2)   # Return 4
pp times2           # Print "[5, 9, 4, 6, 10, 8]"
```

Side effects in Ruby (best-time.rb)

Finally, avoiding side effects allows functions to use an
optimization technique called Memorization. This technique
consists of remembering the value returned by the function the first
time it is called. When the function is called again with the same
parameters, instead of executing the body of the function, the
remembered value is returned. If the function does not produce any
side effects, this technique is perfectly safe because it is guaranteed
that the same input parameters always produce the same result. A

very simple example of memorization in JavaScript is the following implementation of the Fibonacci series:

```javascript
var fibonacciCache = {0: 1, 1: 1};

function fibonacci(pos) {
  if (pos < 0) {
    throw "Fibonacci series is only defined for natural numbers";
  }

  if (! fibonacciCache.hasOwnProperty(pos)) { console.log("I
    calculate the result for the position " + pos);
    fibonacciCache[pos] = fibonacci(pos - 1) + fibonacci(pos -
    2);
  }

  return fibonacciCache [pos];
```

Implementation of the Fibonacci series with memorization (fibonacci.js)

If you copy this code to a JavaScript console (say, Node) and make different calls to the Fibonacci function, you will be able to check (thanks to the messages printed by console.log) that each position in the series is only calculated once.

In dynamic languages such as Python, Ruby, or JavaScript, it is relatively easy to write a function that receives another function as a parameter and applies the "saving" technique to it. The following section explores the technique of manipulating functions as data.

Higher-Order Functions

Another common feature of functional languages is to treat functions as "first-class citizens." That is, functions are more or less normal values that can be passed as parameters, assigned to variables, and returned as a result of a function call. Functions that use this characteristic, that is, that manipulate or return functions, are called higher-level functions. Fortunately, many popular languages have this type of function.

The first time you encounter higher-order functions, you may think that their uses are limited, but they have many applications. On the one hand, we have the functions and methods brought by the standard language, usually list management. On the other hand, we can write our own functions and methods of higher-order, to separate or reuse code more effectively.

Let's look at an example of the first thing in Ruby. Some of the methods in the Array class are given a function as a parameter (in Ruby they are called blocks), which allows you to write fairly compact and expressive code:

```ruby
# Check if all the words have less than 5 letters if
words.all? {|w| w.length < 5 }
    # ...
end

# Check if customer has any pending shipments if
customer.orders.any? {|o| not o.sent? }
    # ...
end

# Get failed subjects for a failed_subjects =
student.subjects.find_all {|s| s.mark < 5 }

# Divide the candidates between those who know more
than # two languages and the others
polyglots, rest = cands.partition {|c| c.languages.length > 2 }

# Get an uppercase version of the words # on the
list
words = ["hoygan", "kiero", "hanime", "gratix"]
shouts = words.map {|w| w.upcase}
```

Higher-Order Methods in Ruby

The equivalent code that would have to be written to achieve the same result without higher-order functions is considerably longer and harder to read. Moreover, if we wanted to do similar operations by varying the condition (say, in one part of the code we want to check if all the words are less than five letters, and in another part we want to check if all the words are composed exclusively of letters, without numbers or other characters), the code would get worse quickly.

Writing our own functions doesn't have to be difficult either, or used in very special cases. They can be as common and simple as the following example in JavaScript:

```javascript
// We want to be able to write the following
code var comicCollection = new
Database('comics');
comicCollection.onAdd(function(comic) {
    console.log("New comic added: " + comic.title);
});
// The following line should print "New comic..." in the console
comicCollection.add({title:  "Batman: The Dark Knight Returns."
                     author: "Frank Miller"});

// The implementation of onAdd can be very simple
Database.prototype.onAdd = function(f) {
    this.onAddFunction = f;
}
// The implementation of add also
Database.prototype.add = function(obj) {
    this.data.push(obj);
    if (typeof(this.onAddFunction) === 'function') {
        this.onAddFunction(obj);
    }
```

Higher-Order Functions in JavaScript

Starting with ECMAScript 5, the Array class adds several higher-order methods that are common in functional programming.

Lazy Evaluation

The last feature of functional languages that we will explore is lazy evaluation. Not many languages include lazy evaluation, but it can be imitated to some extent, and knowing how it works can give us ideas and inspiration when designing our own systems. One of the relatively few languages that include lazy evaluation is Haskell.

Lazy evaluation is about not doing calculations that are not necessary. For example, let's say we write a function that recursively generates a list of 10 elements and another function that calls the first one, but only uses the value of the fourth element. When the second function is executed, Haskell will execute the first one until the fourth element is calculated.

That is: Haskell will not, like most languages, execute the first function until it returns its value (a list of 10 elements); it will only execute the function until the fourth element in the list is generated, which is all it needs to continue running the main program. In this sense, the first function is like a mathematical expression: initially, Haskell does not know the value of the expression and will only calculate the part of it that he needs. In this case, the first four elements.

What is the advantage of lazy evaluation? In most cases, efficiency. In other cases, readability. When we don't have to worry about the memory or CPU cycles used by our function, we can make them return (theoretically) lists or infinite structures, which can be easier to read or implement in some cases. Although it's not a clearer example of lazy assessment readability, understanding the following implementation of the Fibonacci series will clarify the difference from a strict assessment. Note that the function calculates the entire series, that is, an infinite list:

```
fibs = 0 : 1 : zipWith (+) fibs (tail fibs)
```

Implementation of the Fibonacci series at Haskell

Usually, the function is impossible to understand at first glance if we are not familiar with functional programming and lazy evaluation, but several points will help us:

- tail list returns the given list, skipping the first element. That is, if the list is (1 2 3), the tail list is (2 3).

- zipWith calculates, given operation and two lists, a list that has: as a first element, the result of applying the given operation to the first element of the two lists; as a second element, the result of applying the operation to the second element of the two lists; etc. Thus, zipWith called with the sum function, and the lists (1 2 3) and (0 1 5) would result in (1 3 8).

- Each element in the list returned by fibs will be calculated individually and will be available in memory without the need to re-execute the function code.

- So, what happens is:

- Haskell starts to build a list of elements 0 and 1. At this point, fibs =(0 1).

- The third element will be the first element of the zipWith subexpression. To calculate it, and we need the fibs list (for now (0 1), as we only know two elements) and tail fibs (for now (1)). When you add the first element of each of these lists (0 and 1), the result is 1. At this point, fibs =(0 1 1) and the subexpression zipWith ... =(1).

- The fourth element of fibs is the second element of zipWidth   To calculate this, and we will need the second element of fibs and the second element of tail fibs. The second element of tail fibs is the third element of fibs, which we already know because we calculated it in the previous step. Note that no recursive call is necessary because the values we need are already calculated. Lazy evaluation works as a mathematical function: we do not need to recalculate a value if we already know the result. At this point, fibs =(0 1 1 2) and the subexpression zipWith ... =(1 2).

- For the fifth element (the third one in zipWidth), we will need the third and fourth fibs elements, which at this point, we already know because we have calculated them in the previous steps. And so on.

These steps do not run indefinitely: they will run until you get the fibs element you need. That is, if we assign fibs to a variable but never use it, the code will not be executed at all; if we use the value of the third element of the series in some calculation, only the first two steps described above will be executed; and so on. In no case is an attempt made to run fibs until it returns "the full value."

Lazy evaluation can be seen as applying the "memorization" technique automatically to all languages. One possible use is to calculate tables of values that are slow to calculate: in some cases, we could load a pre-calculated table into memory, but the cost can be prohibitive if the table is large or potentially infinite.

Finally, learning new languages, especially from paradigms we are less familiar with, can teach us many things about programming in general. This learning process will make us better programmers, and many of these lessons will be applicable to all the languages we know, not just the languages similar to the one we just learned. In particular, the functional languages are sufficiently accessible and similar to the most popular languages to teach us many useful lessons.:

Chapter 3

Algorithms, Pseudocodes, and Structured Programming

In Chapter 1, it was mentioned that the computer only understands a series of instructions coded in the computer's own machine language. In this language, instructions are a sequence of zeros and ones (binary code), and writing a program directly in this language would be a laborious and tedious task. It is also certain that the process of detecting errors in the code and its correction would be a process that would take us even longer and would give us a good headache.

Fortunately, the first programmers, faced with the problems already mentioned, sought ways to reduce the effort involved in writing programs. The solution they found was to create languages, called high-level languages, whose syntax was more similar to that of human language, allowing the programmer to write programs in a language that is directly understood. It is the same computer that will translate the programs in the high-level code to the machine code using some programs called translators.

Procedure for Creating a Program

The procedure for creating a program that the computer can run is as follows:

Understand the problem being addressed and specify what information will be provided to the program, input data, and what type of information the program will output in response, output data.

- Design the program algorithm that will convert the input data into the output data of the program.

- Encode the algorithm in a high-level language.

- Use a text editor to edit the code. This code is known as the source program.

- Convert the source program to machine code using a compiler This process is called compiling the program. Normally our source code will have syntax errors that the compiler will detect and tell us. We will have to go back to the editor to correct them and repeat step 5 until our code has no syntax errors. The resulting machine code, also called executable code, is a program that the machine can execute.

- Execute the program feeding it with data for which we know the results that the program will give us and compare the results obtained from the program with the expected results. Often the results obtained do not match those expected. This is because our algorithm contains some logic errors that must be found and corrected.

In this chapter, we will study the first two steps of the procedure to create a program. The rest will be seen in the tutorials of the development system used in the course.

Understanding the Problem

For us to solve any problem, in any discipline, not only in computing, but it is also necessary to understand the problem to be solved. Commonly, we begin to propose solutions before we are clear about the problem to be solved. This means that the results obtained are incorrect and we have to look for a new solution.

Also, it should be considered that in practice, problems that are solved using the computer are complex and usually require the work of several people, for long periods. Hence the importance of clearly understanding the problem before devoting resources to solving it.

A fundamental part of understanding a problem is correctly identifying what answers we want the program to provide and what information we need to provide to the program.

Algorithm and Pseudocode

Once the problem is understood, the next point is to establish the sequence of steps needed to obtain the desired responses from that data. This sequence of steps written formally and systematically is known as an algorithm.

A language is required to describe this algorithm. This language should allow us, apart from the description of the steps to solve the problem, to model the representation of the solution. The latter means that from the description of the solution, someone other than the person who wrote the algorithm can arrive at the same solution. Such language is called pseudo-code.

An algorithm written in pseudocode is a set of sentences written following certain syntax or construction rules.

Sentences

The sentences, also called control structures, are constructions to direct the flow of actions that the computer will perform on the data to obtain the results.

There are three types of statements or control structures: The sequential or compound statement, the conditional or selection statement, and the repetitive or iterative statement.

Compound Sentence

A fundamental characteristic of an algorithm is that it is formed by a set of instructions or steps that are executed in a well-defined sequence. This set of instructions that are executed in a sequence is known as a composite statement. Each instruction in a composite statement can be a simple statement, a composite statement, a conditional statement, or a repetitive statement. A simple sentence is an instruction that cannot be broken down into simpler instructions.

In pseudocode, a compound sentence is written by writing each of its compound sentences on a separate line:

sentence1

    [sentence2]...

Note that a composite statement can be made up of one or more statements.

Example of the Composite Judgment

Consider the following problem:

Write the pseudocode for a program that converts a given speed in km/hr to m/s.

We can see that the expected response of this program is a number that represents the speed expressed in m/s. Also, the program has as input a number representing the speed expressed in km/hr. The conversion factor is not an input since its value does not change and can be considered as a constant in the program.

The search for the solution to this problem will be done in several approaches. We will start with a very general solution and refine it in successive approaches. This technique is known as top-down design. The first approach establishes what needs to be done to solve the problem without worrying about how. The following approaches will refine the solution by detailing how. The first approximation of the solution could be the following pseudo-code:

read speed

converts speed from km/hr to m/s

writes speed

The first sentence causes the computer to read a number supplied by the user of the program, which represents the speed in km/hr. That number is stored in a location in the RAM called a variable. Each variable has a name. The variable used in this program is called speed.

The second instruction takes the value of the speed in km/hr and converts it to m/s, leaving the result in the same speed variable and finally the last instruction takes the value of the speed in m/s stored in the speed variable and writes it so that the user knows the result.

Note that the three sentences of the pseudo-code must be executed in the order in which they were written. The computer cannot do the speed conversion until it knows the speed in km/hr. You also cannot write the speed in m/s before you have calculated this speed. These three sentences constitute a composite sentence.

In the following approaches to the solution, each of the steps of the first approach will be refined by trying to express how each of those steps should be performed. In the end, these steps must be expressed in terms of the operations that the computer is capable of performing, which are certain arithmetic and logical operations.

Also, it has already been mentioned that the computer has certain input and output devices through which we can feed it or extract information. Therefore, we can think that the computer can "read" and "write" data and that there must be instructions that tell the computer to perform those functions.

In pseudocode, these instructions are denoted by the keywords: read and write. We can think of it as reading and writing simple sentences. The statement reads, allows the user to supply data through an input device, usually the keyboard, and stores it in a variable. The written statement displays a result on an output device, usually the monitor.

We still have to analyze the second sentence of our pseudocode: Convert the speed from km/hr to m/s. Here we can ask ourselves: Is there an instruction to carry out the conversion of speed in km/hr to m/s? The answer is no. The task of converting speeds, as well as any other conversion, can be expressed from other more elementary tasks. The task of converting speed in km/hr to m/s can be written as:

takes the data stored in the speed variable

multiply it by 1000

divides the previous result by 3600

stores the result in the variable speed

The four steps above can be represented in abbreviated form by the following expression:

speed = speed * 1000/3600

Where the symbol = called assignment operator, means that the original value of the speed variable is to be replaced by the result of:

speed * 1000/3600

That is the result of multiplying (*) the value that is stored in the speed variable by 1000 and dividing (/) by 3600. Then a second approach to the desired program would be given by the following pseudo-code:

read speed

speed = speed * 1000/3600

writes speed

In this program, only two approaches were necessary so that all the steps of the program were instructions that the computer could execute. More complex programs will require more approaches.

Composite Sentence Exercise

Write the pseudocode for a program that reads the three sides of a triangle and writes its area.

Conditional Sentence

A second sentence, the conditional sentence, allows the computer to select between two alternative courses to follow, depending on a given condition. The syntax of the conditional sentence is:

if(expression)

sentence1

[other

sentence2]

If it's a keyword with which you start the conditional sentence. The keyword other separates the two compound sentences: sentence1 and sentence2. The expression in parentheses, when evaluated, can only take the values false or true. If the value of an expression is true, the computer executes sentence1; otherwise, the computer will execute sentence2.

Note that the construction:

[other

sentence2]

It is optional (it is enclosed in square brackets). If it is omitted and the expression value is false, then the computer will do nothing.

We have already mentioned that a composite sentence can be made up of one or more sentences. If the compound sentences of the conditional sentence have only one sentence, they can also be written as follows:

if(*expression*) { *statement11 statement12 ...*

    }

    [other {

            sentence21 sentence22 ...

    }]

Note that keys, {} have delimited the sentences that make sentence1. This tells us that all sentences will be executed if the expression is true. If we skip the keys and write:

if(*expression*) *sentence11 sentence12 ...*

    [other {

            sentence21 sentence22 ...

    }]

The construction is incorrect because if the expression is true, only the sentence would be executed.11 The sentence12 ... would be considered as independent sentences from the conditional sentence and the construction:

    [other

        sentence21 sentence22 ...]

It would no longer be part of the conditional sentence, which is not possible since this construction cannot exist by itself. Also, the sentences that form sentence2 have been delimited by keys to indicate that all sentences will be executed if the expression is false. If we skip the keys and write:

if(*expression*) { *statement11 statement12 ...*

       }

          [other

sentence21 sentence22 ...]

The construction, although correct, will not produce the desired effect since if the expression is false, only the sentence will be executed21. sentence22 ... would be considered as sentences independent of the conditional sentence.

Examples on the Conditional Sentencing

- Write the pseudocode for a program that reads three whole numbers and writes the largest of them.

In this problem, the input data are three positive numbers, a, b and c, and the expected response is a number, the largest of the three. A first approach to solving the problem may be:

read a, b, c

find the largest of a, b and c

senior writer

Where a, b, and c are the variables that contain the input numbers, and the highest is the variable that contains the largest of the three numbers. In this pseudo-code, the only step that needs to be refined is the second, since the first and third correspond to simple sentences. To find the largest of a, b, and c, the computer must compare the three numbers. However, the computer can only compare two numbers at a time. So the second step must be separated into two parts:

find a and b's wholesale and store it

wholesale find c's

wholesale and store it wholesale

To find the largest of a and b, the computer must ask itself: is it larger than b? The following conditional sentence can express this.

if(a > b) greater = a

other major = b

Here the computer evaluates the expression a > b. If it is true, i.e., if a > b, it will assign the value of a to the larger variable. Otherwise, it will store the value of b. However, when the sentence is finished, the greater of a and b will be.

In the same way, to find the highest of c and major, we can use the following conditional sentence.

if(c > major) major = c

If the expression c > major is true, it means that the largest of the three numbers is c, and therefore, we store it in the major variable. Note that in this case, there is no statement 2 since if the expression c > major is false, the major variable already contains the largest of the three numbers, and it is not necessary to change the value of this variable.

The pseudo-code for this program is then like:

    read a, b, c

        if(a > b) greater = a

    other major = b

        if(c > major) major = c

    senior writer

Exercise

Write the pseudo-code of a program, which performs the four fundamental operations of arithmetic. The program should read the first number, the character representing the desired operation, and the second number. The program will display the result.

In this program, the entry will consist of two numbers representing the operands and one character representing the operator. The output will consist of a number representing the result of an error message if the operation is invalid.

The first approach to solving the problem may be:

reads result reads operator reads operand

calculate result

write the result

The first operand is stored in a variable called result, and it is in this variable that the result remains at the end of the program. The operator variable contains the operator (character used to indicate the operation), and the operand variable contains the second of the operands. In this pseudo-code, the only step that needs to be refined is the fourth. The others correspond to simple read and write sentences. How the result is calculated depends on the operation to be performed and is determined by the content of the operator variable. The calculation of the result can be written using the following cascading conditional statements:

if(operator == '+') result = result + operand

other if(operator == '-') result = result - operand other if(operator == '*') result = result * operand other if(operator == '/')

if(operand != 0.0) result = result / operand

another writes "Error: Division by zero"

another writes "Error: Unknown operator"

In the expression of the conditional sentence:

operator == '+'

The == symbol means "equal to,"so the computer asks if the character stored in the operator variable is equal to the '+' character. If this is true, the contents of the result and operand variables will be added together and the result will be stored in the result variable. If not, we investigate whether the desired operation is subtraction, etc.

Note that if the desired operation is division, the value in the variable operand is compared with zero. If the value in operand is not zero, we can do the division; otherwise, we will display an error message since the division by zero is not valid.

The pseudo-code for this program looks like:

    reads result reads operator reads operand

    if(operator == '+') result = result + operand other if(operator
    == '-') result = result - operand other if(operator == '*')
    result = result * operand other if(operator == '/')

    if(operand != 0.0) result = result / operand

    another writes, "Error: Division by zero."

    another writes, "Error: Unknown operator."

write the result

Exercises on the Conditional Sentencing

- The cost of an ordinary telegram is $1000 if the number of words is up to 10; for each additional word, there is a charge of \$200. If the telegram is urgent, the costs are \$2000 and \$400 respectively. Write the pseudo-code for a program that reads the type of the telegram (a single letter, 'O' for ordinary and 'U' for urgent) and the number of words in the telegram and write the cost of the telegram.

- Write the pseudocode for a program that reads three positive numbers supplied in ascending order, which represent the lengths of the sides of a triangle. The program should determine whether the three sides form a triangle and its type.

Repetitive Judgment

The repetitive statement allows the computer to execute a series of steps or instructions repeatedly as long as a given condition is met. The syntax of this sentence is as follows:

    while(expression)

Chapter 4

The Process of Bending & Breaking

The Law of Demeter

The Law of Demeter (LoD) or also the "Principle Of Least Knowledge,""Law of Goodstyle" or "Law of Demeter for Functions/Methods" (LoD-F) was first established in autumn 1987 by Ian Holland at Northeastern University in Boston within the framework of the research project "Demeter"1. According to K. Lieberherr, I. Holland, and A. Riel, the Demeter law is a programming language independent guideline, which takes up the idea of modularization and encapsulation in object-oriented software development.

K. Lieberherr, I. Holland, and A. Riel first formulated the purpose of the Law of Demeter in their 1988 publication with the words "The motivation behind this law is to ensure that the software is as modular as possible... The modularization of software is accompanied by a weak coupling of the individual components, which is why LoD can also be regarded as a special case of design principle- zips loose coupling.

If one speaks of modularity and weak coupling in software development, this presupposes a restriction of the mutual awareness of the individual software components and thus their mutual communication. Karl Lieberherr describes the Principle of Least Knowledge accordingly with the formulation "Each unit should have only limited knowledge about other units: only units closely related to the current unit," with which he establishes a connection to the design principle of information hiding. Lieberherr also restricts communication with the statement, "Each unit should only talk to its friends; Don't talk to strangers." Lieberherr understands a "unit" in connection with the LoD as a method. The confidentiality principle2 is, therefore, of great importance when considering the Law of Demeter. Methods, which can be used with the law of Demeter, only know the internal structure of "friendly" classes. Structural information regarding "foreign" classes remains hidden.

If Lieberherr's statement - to speak only with friends and not with strangers - is transferred to the class constellation shown in the following picture, for example, this has the meaning explained in the following about permitted method calls. Within the method test() of class A, the friendly class B may be accessed via the reference refB and its methods. A call such as refB.doSomethingB() is therefore legitimate because A only talks to his friend B. The following figure shows the constellation of these classes in a class diagram:

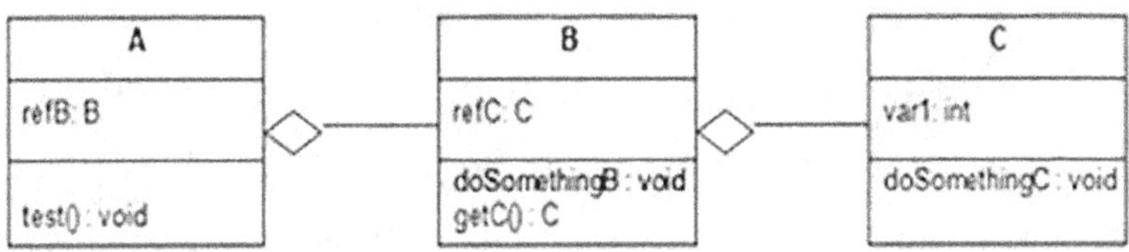

However, if refB.getC().do- SomethingC() is called within the method test(), a class C unknown to class A has accessed across B. The principle of secrecy, and consequently, the law of Demeter is violated by such a call for methods. In the course of the adherence to the design principle information hiding, the LoD drastically limits the permissible concatenation of method calls.

If the knowledge about other components and their structure is to be limited to friends, the communication of two strangers (here A and C) must be encapsulated by an additional method - in class B in between. These methods are also known as wrapper methods3. They enable indirect communication between two, not explicitly friendly objects.

The goal of the Law of Demeter is to reduce dependencies and thus provide a software system with minimal dependencies. Lieberherr, Holland, and Riel have specified which concrete method calls are permitted within the framework of the LoD in various formulations describing different characteristics of the law.

Forms of the Law of Demeter

As with many other principles of design, the Demeter Law also has various forms, interpretations, and stages of development. In 1988 the inventors of the LoD, K. Lieberherr, I. Holland, and A. Riel, distinguished in their publication a "weak Law of Demeter" from a "strong Law of Demeter." The following year, K. Lieberherr and I. Holland, on the other hand, refers to two further categories, an "object form" and a "class form." The following subchapters deal with these characteristics.

Object Shape

The formulation of Demeter's law in the object form is the most commonly used form. Thus, it can also be regarded as a general or general expression of the Law of Demeter. Lieberherr, Holland, and Riel use the object form to define the boundaries within which method calls to objects conform to the Law of Demeter. It is defined which objects can be considered as friends. The following definition of the object shape is based on .

A method m of an object : A may only call the following methods after the LoD:

- Methods of the object: A itself,

- Methods of the objects passed to m,

- Methods of objects newly created locally in A and

- Methods of a global4 object of A.

The following program code shows this with concrete examples in the programming language Java:

```java
public class MyLawOfDemeter {
  private A aRef = new A();
  private void doSomething() {}

  public void testMethod(B bRef) {
    C cRef = new C();
    this.doSomething();    // (1) -> current class
    bRef.doSomething();    // (2) -> argument class
    cRef.doSomething();    // (3) -> immediate part class
    aRef.doSomething();    // (4) -> immediate part class
  }
}
```

Along with this, Lieberherr also describes the Law of Demeter with the words " you should only talk to yourself (current class), to close relatives (immediate part classes), and friends who visit you (argument classes)." A further concatenation such as a Ref.getD().doSomething() within the method testMethod() of the class MyLawOfDemeter would violate the law of Demeter. Because an object of class D, which would be returned by getD(), is not known to the current class. The class MyLawOfDemeter would, therefore, "talk" to the "stranger" D, which is not allowed.

Class Form

The class shape is very similar to the object shape but is not only applied to objects, but to entire classes in general. Here a distinction is made between a minimized and a strict form. The following definitions of strict and minimized forms are based on and.

Strict Form: A method m of class A may call the following methods:

- Methods of class A itself,

- Methods of the class of a transfer parameter of m,

- Methods of classes whose instances were created locally, or

- Methods of a class of a global6 object.

- Minimized Form: The minimized form loosens the restrictions of the strict form a little. It allows access to methods of further classes, namely

- A class that is stable or implements a stable interface7,

- A class whose methods require direct access for reasons of runtime efficiency, or

- A class of a newly created object.

This form of the LoD is the weakest form of the law and thus brings with it the fewest restrictions for permitted method calls.

Weak Law of Demeter

The "weak Law of Demeter" was defined in 1988 by K. Liebherr, I. Holland, and A. Riel as follows:

"The Weak Law of Demeter defines instance variables as being BOTH the instance variables that make up a given class AND any instance variables inherited from other classes."

This means that a class can access both its own instance variables and the variables inherited from the base class within methods. If the weak Law of Demeter is applied, changes in the base class also affect the methods of derived classes, which directly use these base class objects affected by changes.

Strong Law of Demeter

While the weak Law of Demeter allows methods to access inherited variables, the strong Law of Demeter restricts access to inherited variables.

"The Strong Law of Demeter defines instance variables as being ONLY the instance variables that make up a given class. Inherited instance variable types may not be passed messages."

According to the strong Law of Demeter, a variable is only called an instance variable if it is a direct component of the class under consideration. Access in a method of a derived class to a variable that has been passed on to the derived class by inheritance is not legitimate. Therefore, the strong Law of Demeter often requires additional methods (wrapper methods), which encapsulate the dependence of the methods of the derived classes on the concrete structure of the base class.

These wrapper methods act as intermediaries between the attributes of the base class and the methodologies of the derived class. It is important that they are implemented in the base class and not overwritten by the derived classes. If the internal structure - for example, the attributes - of the base class is changed, this only affects the corresponding wrapper method, but not the methods of the derived classes.

This form of the LoD thus supports the principle of information hiding more strongly than the Weak Law of Demeter and thus reduces the dependencies between a base class and its derived classes.

Example for the Weak and Strong Law of Demeter

K. Lieberherr, I. Holland, and A. Riel explain the difference between strong and weak LoD in "Object-Oriented Programming: An Objective Sense of Style" using a fruit basket as an example. In this case, there is a single apple, a single orange, and a single plum in each fruit basket (class fruit basket). The classes apple, orange, and plum, are derived from the class fruit, which has an attribute weight.

Different formulas are needed to calculate the weight of the different fruits in the fruit basket, as the actual fruit content varies according to variety. For example, in the case of a plum, the weight of the pit must be deducted, and in the case of an orange, the weight of the skin. The weight of each individual fruit variety should be determined using the corresponding formula.

If the weak law of Demeter is applied, the classes Apple, Orange and Plum each have their own method called calculate a weight(), which calculates the weight using the attribute weight and a percentage inherited from the class Fruit. The following example shows the implementation of the class Fruit, the class Fruit Basket and exemplary for a concrete fruit, the class Apple, considering the weak LoD:

```
public abstract class Fruit{ float Weight = 1.0f; public
Fruit(){};

        public abstract float calculate weight();

}
```

```java
public class apple extends fruit{ public float calculate
weight() {

        return Weight*0.85f;

        }

}

public class fruit basket {

private ArrayList<fruit>fruit = new ArrayList<fruit>();

private float fruit basketWeight = 0; public fruit basket(){

fruits.add(new apple());

...

}

public float calculate weight() { for (fruit elem : fruits){

fruit basketWeight += elem.calculateWeight();

        }

                return fruit basket weight;

        }

}
```

```java
public abstract class Fruit{ float Weight = 1.0f; public
Fruit(){};

        public abstract float calculate weight();

}

public class apple extends fruit{ public float calculate
weight() {

                return Weight*0.85f;

        }

}

public class fruit basket {

private ArrayList<fruit>fruit = new ArrayList<fruit>();
private float fruit basketWeight = 0;

        public fruit basket(){   fruit.add(new apple());

        ...

}

public float calculate weight() { for (fruit elem : fruits){

        fruit basketWeight += elem.calculateWeight();

}
```

return fruit basket weight;

    }

  }

Access by the derived class Apple to the attribute weight of the basic class Fruit is not permitted after the strong LoD. If the strong LoD is followed, a wrapper method (calculate-percentage-weight()), which is located in the base class and called by the derived classes, encapsulates the access to the attribute weight. The derived classes now do not have precise information about the implementation of the method or the attributes of the base class.

The following program code shows the implementation of the fruit basket example in compliance with the strong Law of Demeter:

```
public abstract class Fruit {float Weight = 1.0f;


        public fruit () {};

public abstract float calculate weight ();

        public float calculate percentage weight (float
        percentage) {return weight * percent;

        }


    }
```

```java
public class apple extends fruit {public float calculate
weight () {

        return this.calculatePercentageWeight (0.85f);

        }

}

public class fruit basket {

private ArrayList <fruit> fruit = new ArrayList <fruit> ();
private float fruit basketWeight = 0;

        public fruit basket () {fruit.add (new apple ());

        ...

}

public float calculate weight () {for (fruit elem: fruits) {

        fruitbasketWeight  +  =  elem.calculateWeight  ();
        System.out.println (fruit basket weight);

        }

                return fruit basket weight;

        }

}
```

Advantages

The law of Demeter helps developers to create robust and well-structured software. In combination with the minimization of code duplication, the number of passing parameters of methods, and the number of methods of a class, a lower coupling of methods and increased "information hiding" is achieved. This leads to independent interchangeability, testability and reusability of the individual software components and easier maintenance of the complete software.

By decoupling the relationships across several classes, the complexity of the methods can be reduced, and the comprehensibility of the software can be achieved through greater proximity to reality. This is the case with David Bock's Paperboy, for example. No customer would hand the paperboy his wallet so that he could take his own wages.

At the method level, the LoD leads to so-called narrow interfaces, since each method only needs to know about a small number of methods of the friendly objects.

In addition, the Law of Demeter covers other design principles, such as loose coupling and information hiding.

Disadvantages

Due to the prohibition to talk to strangers, additional methods - wrapper methods - are often necessary to implement the desired functionality. These methods often require a large number of transfer parameters.

In addition, the Demeter law leads to so-called wide interfaces on class level, because, as already mentioned, compliance with the LoD requires additional helper methods, the wrapper methods, to avoid nesting through object structures.

Accordingly, powerful interfaces at the class level may be problematic because they violate some design principles of software development, such as the interface segregation principle, the single responsibility principle, or separation of concerns.

The implementation of software in compliance with the Demeter law can also lead to a slight loss of performance or a slightly increased memory requirement.

The law of Demeter, like most software design principles, deals with the reduction of dependencies. It tries to eliminate these dependencies by prohibiting certain method accesses. Thus, a software system developed under LoD benefits from a better structuring, which results in a reduction of dependencies and also greatly increases clarity, maintainability, and testability. Appropriately, the law of Demeter is often called the Law of Goodstyle.

With the statement, " any object-oriented program written in bad style can be transformed systematically into a structured program obeying the Law of Demeter. 1, p. 324] Lieberherr, Holland, and Riel show that the Law of Demeter can be applied to any bad software design in general with success.

The Law of Demeter cannot generally be regarded as universally applicable and incontestable. It should rather be understood as a kind of guideline, which is, if possible. However, there are also cases in which the application of the LoD is not appropriate. For example, if the requirements for the performance have a higher priority than, for example, maintainability or adaptability.

The concrete implementation of the Demeter law varies depending on the programming language used. Lieberherr, Holland, and Riel, therefore, formulated the LoD separately for different programming languages (Smalltalk-80, CLOS, Eiffel, and C++). In programming languages that use a dot or an arrow as an access operator to components such as methods or attributes (e.g., Java, C++), the LoD is often limited to the simple rule of using only a dot or arrow. A transfer of the Law of Demeter to the Java programming language is missing in the original form wrestling.

For this reason, in this section, we tried to transfer the LoD to Java in the sense of the inventors as an example.

What Is Metaprogramming?

Metaprogramming or metaprogramming as we say in English, is one of the most challenging terms that a developer can find, in short, we usually think of metaprogramming as the ability to use code to generate code, the problem is that I can go from, with metaprogramming I can generate code to effectively take advantage of the implementation of metaprogramming of a language, there is a long way.

What We Use Metaprogramming For?

First let's try to understand why the concept is important, in the end, it is likely that until now you have survived without a code routine that generates more code, in the end, that code can also be written by us, right?

id	title	duration
one	Ruby course	1500
two	Laravel course	200
3	JavaScript course	900

Consider that we have a Courses table, which has a title and duration, in previous versions of Rails, it was possible to use a method like the following to search for items in the table:

```
def search_courses

    Course.find_by_title_and_duration('Ruby',100)

End
```

The question is, where do these methods come from? It's not possible for the framework developers to define a method for each combination of fields in a program. The answer is metaprogramming.

Now, consider Ruby's next program:

```ruby
class HTML

  def self.method_missing(nomb_method, *args, &block)

    tag(nomb_method,*args,&block)

  end

  def self.tag(tag_name,*args,&block)

"<#{tag_name}>#{args.last} #{yield if block_given?}</#{tag_name}>"

  end

end
```

It is used as follows:

```ruby
html = HTML.div do

HTML.header do

  HTML.h1 "Titulo de la pagina"

end +

HTML.article do
```

    HTML.p "Hola a todos"

 end

end

puts html

The result of this program is as follows:

<div>

<header>

<h1>Titulo de la pagina </h1>

</header>

<article>

<p>Hola a todos </p>

</article>

</div>

Note how each label is a method, did I have to define them all? No, I used metaprogramming.

You can run the program on your own in the following console:

```
class HTML
```

```ruby
    def self.method_missing(nomb_method, *args,
&block)

        tag(nomb_method,*args,&block)

    end

    def self.tag(tag_name,*args,&block)

        "<#{tag_name}>#{args.last} #{yield if
block_given?}</#{tag_name}>"

    end

end

html = HTML.div do

    HTML.header do

        HTML.h1 "Titulo de la pagina"

    end +

    HTML.article do

        HTML.p "Hola a todos"

    end

end
```

    puts html

    ruby 2.5.5p157 (2019-03-15 revision 67260) [x86_64-linux]

Well used, metaprogramming allows us to create dynamic and expressive applications, misused, metaprogramming can be transformed into a black box that delivers erroneous results, and nobody understands why.

Using Metaprogramming

Something very important that you need to know is that each language has different implementations of metaprogramming, and that the line that separates metaprogramming from dynamic code is very diffuse, what some consider metaprogramming, others do not. So, keep that in mind.

Executing Strings As Code

One of the simplest forms of metaprogramming is a function that receives a string and evaluates it as a code; in JavaScript, we have the eval function.

    eval('console.log(2+2)')); // Imprime 4 en console.

Just like JavaScript, many languages have an implementation of the eval function. Considering that with code, we can build a chain, eval becomes the simplest form of metaprogramming, we generate code, store it in a chain, and execute it. Although it is metaprogramming, I will not be the first to tell you that this kind of function should be treated with care, they are generally prone to leave security breaches, or the performance of the code executed is slower.

Introspection And Reflection

Other forms of metaprogramming are introspection and reflection, related concepts that represent more elegant forms of metaprogramming.

Introspection is the quality of a language to answer the question What am I? When a language, through APIs and methods, can give you information about what is happening, that is called introspection. Introspection, such as is not metaprogramming; in the end, we are only being given information.

Introspection becomes metaprogramming when, based on the information provided, we make decisions that affect program execution. Almost all languages have ways to evaluate the current state of the code; in Ruby, for example, we can use the methods method that gives us an array with all the object's methods.

```
# Returns all methods that integers have (numbers)

2.methods
```

JavaScript has several methods in the Object object that fits in the introspection category, such as getOwnPropertyNames, keys, is Frozen, and many simpler expressions such as type of that returns the type of the object can be considered introspection.

```
Object.getOwnPropertyNames ({}) // Returns the properties of the object
```

type of "hello" // Returns the type of the data, in this case, string

Reflection, on the other hand, is the ability to alter the information of the elements of language, unlike the introspection that only gives us information; with reflection, we alter this information.

Separating the modifications that are considered reflection and those that are not, is very simple, the information that is modified with reflection is the metadata, that is, descriptive data from the data, what it means is that if I modify an object that stores a number, I am modifying the data:

```
// This is not reflection

let number = 20;

number = 10;
```

On the other hand, if I modify the container of that data, I am modifying the data of the data. It looks like a pun, doesn't it? A simpler example is that of photography, the data of a photograph is the pixels that build it, while metadata are details that describe the image, such as the location in which it was taken. This is what happens with the programs.

Examples of reflections with more complex, consider Ruby, for example. The base language behavior tells us that the following expression will give us 4.

```
#Return 4, a simple sum
```

$$2 + 2$$

But what if not. In Ruby, we can modify the behavior of operations like this, and the code would look like this:

```ruby
class Integer

  def +(value)

    self * value

  end

end



  puts 2 +3
```

What do you think the previous code will print? Check it out in the following interactive console:

```ruby
class Integer

  def +(value)

    self * value

  end

end

  puts 2 +3
```

ruby 2.5.5p157 (2019-03-15 revision 67260) [x86_64-linux]

Even if you don't believe it, print 6 since we modify the sum operator so that instead of adding it, it multiplies. This is a reflection because we modify the container, the Integer class.

Of course, there is no point in modifying the behavior of the integers, but the message is the same; we modify the behavior so that it behaves differently; that is what we call reflection.

A more practical example is to create a class that can be iterated (run through a cycle) so that you control how your structure will run when you place it in the cycle. Below is an example of JavaScript.

```javascript
class Document{

constructor(content){

this.content = content;

}

[Symbol.iterator](){

let index = 0;

let words = this.content.split("");

return{

next: ()=>{
```

```javascript
        let currentValue = words[index++];

        return {value:currentValue, done:index >
words.length};

    }

    }

    }

    }
```

This class is iterable and can be placed in a cycle as you see below:

```javascript
let doc = new Document("Hello world how are you");

    for(let word of doc) {

        console.log(word);

    }
```

There are many advanced things here, and the important thing is that you perceive how we made our Document object work within a for-of loop, giving personalized behavior to the iteration of an object, in this case, that it traveled through the word by word cycle our structure Document.

You can play with this example in the following console:

```javascript
class Document{
```

```javascript
    constructor(content){

    this.content = content;

    }

    [Symbol.iterator](){

      let index = 0;

      let words = this.content.split("");

       return{

         next: ()=>{

           let currentValue = words[index++];

           return    {value:currentValue,    done:index    >
words.length};

     }

      }

    }

  }

  let doc = new Document("Hello world how are you ");

  for(let word of doc) {console.log(word); }
Native Browser JavaScript
```

Part of how a language allows us to implement Metaprogramming is exposing the internal parts of the language so that we can manipulate and control them, that's where hindsight comes into play.

With this, we cover three different forms of metaprogramming, the execution of code via a string, which, as we discuss, is the simplest but not the most efficient, professional, or used.

Introspection and reflection, which through the exposure of metadata of the language and its modification, allow us to alter how a program is executed, offering us greater control to make code more readable and dynamic.

These are not the only concepts, and we also have the MonkeyPatching, the Templates in C ++ and many more, remember that each language decides to implement this methodology differently.

Temporary Coupling
What is Temporary Coupling?
Temporal Coupling is a code smell that is sometimes not given the attention it deserves. An internet search serves to verify that you don't write much about it. Basically, it consists of having a method that requires the execution of a second method before it can be executed.

For example:

```
<? php
```

```php
namespace  Solid \ Infrastructure \ Service ;

class  mailer

{

    private  $ server ;

    private  $ port ;

    private  $ user ;

    private  $ password ;

    private  $ connection ;

    public  function  __construct ( $ server , $ port , $ user , $
password )

        {

            $ this -> server  =  $ server ;

            $ this -> port  =  $ port ;

            $ this -> user  =  $ user ;

            $ this -> password  =  $ password ;

        }

    public  function  init ()

        {
```

```php
        $this -> connection = new Connection (

            $this -> server ,

            $this -> port ,

            $this -> user ,

            $this -> password

        );

    }

    public function sendEmail ( $subject , $body , $recipient )

    {

        if ( null === $this -> connection ) {

            throw new ServiceNotAvailableException ();

        }


        $this -> connection -> send ( $subject , $body , $recipient );

    }

}
```

In this case, we cannot execute the method sendEmailwithout first calling the method init; therefore, there is a temporary coupling between the method sendEmail and the method init.

This coupling also makes us not intuitive to use this class, since it would be logical to have the class already initialized.

A very simple solution for this case would be to make the init private method and call it from the constructor, leaving the object already initialized correctly:

```php
<? php

namespace  Solid \ Infrastructure \ Service ;

class  mailer

{

    private  $ server ;

    private  $ port ;

    private  $ user ;

    private  $ password ;

    private  $ connection ;


        public  function  __construct ( $ server , $ port , $ user , $
    password )
```

```php
    {
        $this -> server = $ server ;

        $this -> port = $ port ;

        $this -> user = $ user ;

        $this -> password = $ password ;


        $this -> init ();

    }


    private function init ()
    {
        $this -> connection = new Connection (

            $this -> server ,

            $this -> port ,

            $this -> user ,

            $this -> password

        );
```

```php
        }


    public function sendEmail ( $ subject , $ body , $
recipient )

        {

        $ this -> connection -> send ( $ subject , $ body , $
recipient );

        }

    }
```

Temporary Coupling in Dependency Injection

When we talk about dependency investment and dependency injection, we talk about two ways to inject dependencies:

- Via builder

- Via setters

As I said, injection through setters can create a temporary link with the methods that make use of the dependency:

```php
<? php

namespace  Solid \ ApplicationService ;

class  RegisterUserApplicationService

{
```

```php
    private $ repository ;


    public function setRepository ( UserRepositoryInterface
$ repository )
    {
        $ this -> repository = $ repository ;

    }


    public function execute ( $ email , $ password )
    {
        $ user = new User ( $ email , $ password );


        if ( null === $ this -> repository ) {
            throw new RepositoryNotSetException ();

        }


        $ this -> repository -> save ( $ user );

    }

}
```

In this case, if, after instantiating the service, we do not inject the repository, we will not be able to register the user without obtaining an exception in return.

Here we can consider two solutions:

- Inject the dependency into the constructor (my preferred option)

- Inject the dependency directly into the coupled method.

This second solution is simple to implement, but personally, I prefer that the dependencies are resolved in the constructor:

```php
<? php

namespace  Solid \ ApplicationService ;

class  RegisterUserApplicationService

{

    public  function  execute ( $ email , $ password ,
UserRepositoryInterface  $ repository )

    {

        $ user  =  new  User ( $ email , $ password );


        $ repository -> save ( $ user );

    }

}
```

Other Solutions to Temporary Coupling

In summary, we have seen three possible solutions to temporal coupling:

- Remove the dependency on the constructor

- Inject the dependency directly into the constructor

- Inject the dependency into the dependent method

But we still have a possible solution, which sometimes improves the readability of the code, in addition to eliminating the coupling. It consists of merging the dependent methods into a single method and making the others private.

```php
<? php

namespace  Solid \ Repository ;

class  UserRepository

{

    private  $ validated  =  false ;


    public  function  save ( User  $ user )

    {

        if ( ! $ this -> validated ) {

            throw  new  UserNotValidatedException ();

        }
```

```php
        $ this -> repository -> save ( $ user );

        $ this -> validated  =  false ;

    }


    public  function  validate ( User  $ user )

        {

        // validation logic

        $ this -> validated  =  true ;

        }

    }
```

In this case, we can generate a single method called validateAndSave that combines both logics, and since they are dependent on each other, it would be logical to leave the methods save and validates private.

The result is a semantically more correct method without dependencies:

```php
<? php

namespace  Solid \ Repository ;

class  UserRepository

    {

    private  $ validated  =  false ;
```

```php
private function save ( User $ user )
{
    if ( ! $ this -> validated ) {

        throw new UserNotValidatedException ();

    }


    $ this -> repository -> save ( $ user );

    $ this -> validated = false ;

}


private function validate ( User $ user )
{
    // validation logic

    $ this -> validated = true ;

}


public function validateAndSave ( User $ user )
{
    $ this -> validate ( $ user );

    $ this -> save ( $ user );

}
```

Although a priori, it may seem strange to find a temporary link in our code, we must pay attention to the dependencies between methods to avoid falling into this error.

These errors are sometimes complicated to find since sometimes the exceptions are not very descriptive and do not notify us of this dependence. A descriptive message in the exception could simplify this. For example, if it calls init() before sending an email would be enough to know where the shots go; Service not available instead, it can mean a thousand things.

Now that you know more about the temporary link, avoid it using the methods we've seen.

Chapter 5

In The Time of Coding

Programming by Coincidence

What is Programming by Coincidence?

A very common practice in programming is to try to solve problems immediately, without an analysis. The debugger is executed, or the logs are read, and immediately after the problem line is searched, some magic passes, and by magic, the problem is solved. Is there a null object in the middle of my method? With an, if the problem is fixed.

Are you trying to read a directory that does not exist? Ready! With some lines that add the directory, if it does not exist is more than enough. But have you ever thought about whether this is beneficial for your systems? This practice of programming to solve the error, without analyzing the cause, is known as programming by coincidence. Below I explain more:

Each Line of Your System is Acquired Knowledge

All the lines of code in your systems represent knowledge acquired about how the company works or should work. It is important to know how each unit works, and it is more important to understand how the whole works. In large or very old systems through which many programmers have already passed, this knowledge has already been lost. This is a symptom of decline in programs, but it is also a symptom of decline in practices as programmers. If understanding the whole system is representing a great mental effort. It means that the design and architecture of the system are not achieving its objective. You have to make changes, both in the code and in the practices.

The Importance of Context When Coding

Solving a problem out of context is a dangerous activity. Your systems should group concerns and responsibilities. If you must apply some lines of code three layers below to fix the error in a method, then. You are distributing and multiplying your problems instead of solving them. Not to mention that these additional lines can have an unwanted effect on the entire system. Programming by coincidence is usually accompanied by few or no regression tests. Each problem must be solved in the context that the error is caused, only truly exceptional cases, counting on the fingers of your hand should be solved in external contexts.

If you don't know why something doesn't work, much less will you know why it works? Learn before modifying your code.

Modifying complex systems must be a surgical task. You must have certain preparations before touching a single line of code. It is not enough to repair the bug. You have to make sure you leave the code as you found it. And by this, I mean the same functional state. You will need to learn which states are correct and which are incorrect. It is very seductive to repair an obvious problem. A quick repair of a case that was reported to you can cause serious, productive problems if you are not sure how that piece of code should work initially. And I remind you that the moment you modify a component, it is common practice to become directly responsible. Unit and regression tests are your best allies for these cases.

Sometimes You Have to Program by Coincidence

You can't always do things right. You may have limited resources, or a short time, you may not control all system components. This practice is not bad, and I will not demonize. Like all the resources you have as a programmer, it is another tool of the belt. It has consequences that must be evaluated before using it. If short and long term risks are understood and accepted. So, there is nothing wrong with using it, and you just have to remember something.

Programming by coincidence will not serve to leave something terminated. It is a temporary solution. If you are forced to program by coincidence, even if you have solved the problem, this does not mean that the matter should be terminated. You have only bought time; you must continue with the investigation, codify tests. If even looking in every corner of your project, you cannot find the cause.

Leave the case documented so that the next to find the problem does not rediscover the wheel.

Refactoring

When you sit in front of a position to develop a new functionality, in principle, always try to get your code of the highest quality possible. The first problem we encounter is what we understand by quality. You have probably read many software quality articles that relate quality to the number of errors the software presents. True, it is important that our software does not fail, but it is clear that being very important, we need other features to know if the software is of quality. And I am sure that on some occasions and reading the code of an application that we were asked to modify, we have been able to verify that it was very improved even if it did not fail.

That is why coding standards have emerged that make our developments more readable and patterns that allow problems to be solved elegantly and simply that can lead to really complicated solutions. And in this sense, simplicity and clarity are important characteristics of quality. Achieving that simplicity and clarity is complicated:

It is easy to have a complicated idea.

It is very, very complicated to have a simple idea.

- Carver Mead

But the bosses have some problems. It is very easy to apply over-engineering to our developments by trying to apply patterns that would not be necessary. The patterns in many cases teach us to face general design problems, but they do not help us to face the problems of finer detail, such as when our method has too many parameters, or when it would be better to eliminate an inheritance that is not justified, etc.

Trying to define quality may be too ambitious, but we can start from a series of rules that will bring us closer to our quality objective. One of the best rule enumerations is that made by Kent Beck.

- The test suite of the functionality of our software works correctly.

- There is no duplicate code.

- The code allows for the understanding of the design.

- Minimize the number of Classes and Methods.

To achieve this goal, we have two possibilities. One is to get our design to respect all these rules or to try to make our design constantly evolve towards these rules. Refactoring involves applying the second approach that is based on spending time during development to think that we have to change or modify so that our development is of higher quality. It is similar to the procedure we apply in Mathematics when we try to reduce our formulas to make them easier. It is possible that the first design is not the best and having a design and its development in mind that we can improve it.

Refactoring is not a new concept, and we are probably already applying refactoring in our projects; however, it is important to apply it methodically and to know the types of refactoring that are currently being defined.

Refactoring is the process of modifying the code of development to improve its internal structure without altering the functionality offered by the development externally.

Refactoring is one of the practices included in Extreme Programming. To start Refactoring, it is essential that there is a development and that this development has an associated test code that allows us to know at any time, passing automatic tests if the development continues to meet the requirements is implemented.

If these tests do not exist, it will be really complicated to carry out refactoring since we will not be able to know if our modifications have made the development stop working. But that will not only affect us at the time of Refactoring, without or also at the time of trying to modify our development to add new functionality, since we will not know if the newly added code has been able to influence the development to stop working in others cases.

If we do not have evidence, we will probably adopt defensive positions ("If it works, do not touch it"), given the risk of modifying the software, the greater the development. The problem of the tests is that they are not usually automated and that they are usually left in the last place with what they usually do in many cases, not done exhaustively.

Discussing how to face the development of the tests would be another issue, but it is necessary to know what to carry out a refactoring process during development, we will need the tests to be carried out as it develops (Test Development Driven).

Assuming our code has proof, the next step is to know when we should apply the refactoring. Generally, it is a reactive process and generally a consequence of detecting that our code is not of the quality or that it would need restructuring to allow new functionality.

For this reason, refactoring is usually applied when adding a new functionality when we realize that if we restructure the existing code, it would be much easier to add such functionality. However, if we do it constantly by applying it when we detect that our code indicates poor quality (such as duplicate code, for example), we will verify that we are getting our code to be of high quality.

To know if our code needs refactoring, we can check the list of "Bad Smells." A Bad Smell is an indication that there is poor quality code. In the Martin Fowler book (Refactoring: Improving the Design of Existing Code), there is a list of Bad Smells.

Once the Bad Smell has been identified, we must apply a refactoring that allows us to correct this quality problem that we have detected. There are tools in Ant, such as checkstyle, that allow you to automate the identification of these Bad Smell. Examples of Bad Smells are that a method has a large number of lines of code, or has a large number of parameters.

When applying refactoring, we can use the features offered by IDE. The latest versions of development environments offer automatic refactoring that simplifies refactoring. They usually offer the name change of classes, methods, code extraction to a new method, and many more refactoring.

The problem of addressing refactoring is that it is an effort that is not compensated by any new functionality, and for that reason, it is easy not to make. However, if we introduce refactoring as one of the practices that we must apply throughout the development when we finish each functionality, it is one of the best ways to get our code to be of quality, and the experience says that this time we are using in each functionality, It will be more than recovered as the project progresses.

Software Metrics: Cyclomatic Complexity

One of the goals of professional software development is to create high-quality code. From the developer's point of view, this means, among other things, that software becomes readable, testable, and maintainable through a correspondingly good structure. This also brings advantages from the customer's perspective. Maintenance efforts are reduced, and effort estimates for extensions and refactoring are made easier.

In this context, quality cannot remain an empty term under which everyone involved imagines something different. That is why one tries to quantify quality and the observance of quality specifications with the help of software metrics and to make them measurable.

According to the definition of the IEEE A software metric [...], a function that maps a software unit into a numerical value. This calculated value can be interpreted as the degree of fulfillment of a quality property of the software unit.

In this section, I now want the metric cyclomatic complexity, hereafter called CC) to introduce closer. It was introduced in 1976 by Thomas J. McCabe, which is why it is often called the McCabe metric. It specifies the number of different paths through which a software module (e.g., a class or a method in Java) can be run. Formally speaking, when calculating the CC value, the number of binary branches of the control flow graph is simply determined.

Many possible paths mean a high degree of complexity. High complexity usually makes source code more difficult to understand and test. As a result, there is a risk that serious errors will creep into the code during development.

It is, therefore, worthwhile to keep an eye on the CC value. If you draw the right conclusions from this, you can later save a lot of effort for tests and troubleshooting. McCabe specified a value of 10 at that time, which should not be exceeded within a program. Code artifacts that exceed this value should be refactored.

Example: Iteration Over Strings

Using the example of two simple Java methods, the facts will now be illustrated a little. To determine the CC value at the method level, add up as follows:

- Each method has a basic value of 1.

- +1 for each if, while, do, for, ?:, catch, case.

- +1 for each occurrence of the operators &&or||

Applied to Listing 1, the CC value is 5. In Listing 2, this value was reduced to an average value of 2.5 by a few simplifications.

+ Expand source code

Listing 1: Method iterateComplex()with a CC value of 5

+ Expand source code

Listing 2: 2 new methods with an average CC value of 2.5

In Listing 2, the CC value was halved. Outsourcing functionalities achieved this. One method was broken down into two less complex methods. To check a string to avoid a NullpointerException, a utility class from the Apache Commons collection is used in Listing 2.

Application in Practice

The example above was deliberately chosen to be very simple. In practice, the source code is usually much more complex. A certain degree of complexity cannot normally be avoided in non-trivial projects. In addition, the scope of the software is usually so high that it cannot be analyzed without special tools.

With the use of tools such as sonar, however, it is easy to continuously analyze large amounts of source code to then take a closer look at the code artifacts with the greatest complexity. There are usually good candidates for refactoring. According to the motto divide and conquer, complex source code can then be divided into several, easier-to-use segments. Software metrics help to improve the quality of software in a targeted manner and to make the complexity of the source code more manageable.

For some more theoretical background, continue reading the rest of the chapter below.

Many standards for the development of security-critical software require control of the complexity of the software. McCabe's cyclomatic complexity is often used to determine them. However, the thoughtless use of this metric is tricky.

What Cyclomatic Complexity Really Says

As we already know that the cyclomatic complexity (CC) is a measure from graph theory and is based on the control flow graph of a piece of software, for example, a function in the sense of C. The cyclomatic complexity $V (G)$ of a control flow graph is calculated according to the formula $V (G) = e - n + 2$ calculated.

In this formula, e stands for the number of (directed) edges and n for the number of nodes. The formula applies to a coherent control flow graph. The CC of a control flow graph is the number of linearly independent, complete paths through the graph.

The cyclomatic complexity of a control flow graph is also the number of binary (two-valued) decisions plus one. If there are n-valued decisions in the control flow diagram, the n-valued decisions count as n-1 binary decisions. Switch instructions with n case jump labels, each with a subsequent statement block followed by a break, count as n-1 binary decisions. There is also a binary decision for the default label, regardless of whether it is explicitly programmed or not.

The relationship between the cyclomatic complexity V (G) and the number of binary decisions can be illustrated as follows: The control flow graph of a C function without branching consists of two nodes, the start node and the end node, and a directed edge in between.

There is exactly one path through the graph. The cyclomatic complexity for this is V (G) = 1 - 2 + 2 = 1. If you insert a binary decision in the control flow graph, another linearly independent path results, and thus the CC increases by one. Each additional binary decision added also increases the cyclomatic complexity by one.

Values With Little Meaning

You have to be aware that the value of cyclomatic complexity says little about the complexity of software, such as a C function. This can be seen in the following three examples: The cyclomatic complexity does not take into account whether a decision is composed or not.

In the figure below, the func1 () and func2 () functions have the same cyclomatic complexity as the value 2 because they also have the same control flow graph. The fact that the decision in the if statement in the func1 () function is an atomic decision, but that the decision in the if statement in the func2 () function is a decision made up of conditions using logical operators plays a role in the value of the cyclomatic complexity not matter.

Switch instructions are often quite clear for human viewers because they are clearly structured. However, their cyclomatic complexity is high. In the illustration on the next double-page, a switch instruction is shown on the left-hand side, which the human viewer can grasp and understand at a glance. However, the cyclomatic complexity is high, with a value of more than 10.

Calculations do not add to the cyclomatic complexity. The sine () function is shown on the right-hand side of this figure, which performs extensive calculations. Apart from the function name, it is difficult for a human viewer to see what the function is calculating, let alone check whether it does it correctly.

Here, too, there is a large discrepancy between the value of cyclomatic complexity, which is 2, and the functionality that is difficult to understand for humans. Assignments or inputs and outputs also do not increase the cyclomatic complexity, although they make it difficult for people to understand the software.

To avoid these misjudgments, it is advisable to stick to the second determination method of cyclomatic complexity. According to this, the CC is the number of binary decisions plus one. However, this value should not be over-interpreted. High cyclomatic complexity only means many binary decisions, and low cyclomatic complexity means a few binary decisions.

What Cyclomatic Complexity Says?

What can actually be derived from the value of cyclomatic complexity is the maximum number of test cases that are required to achieve 100 percent branch coverage. The CC specifies the number of linearly independent paths through the code. More test cases are, therefore, not necessary to execute all directed edges (the branches) at least once. In this respect, the cyclomatic complexity can be used to estimate the test effort to achieve 100 percent branch coverage.

Tools are required to determine the cyclomatic complexity of real programs. Such tools determine the cyclomatic complexity metric as part of the static analysis of the software. Amazingly, not all tools measure the same values for the same program pieces. Experiments with the commercial tools TESSY, DAC, and Klocwork, as well as the freely available tool CCCC, sometimes result in different values for the examples discussed.

TESSY is a tool for dynamic unit and integration testing of embedded software. The cyclomatic complexity is also determined as a waste product in the analysis of the test object. DAC (Development Assistant for C) is an integrated development environment with the editor, graphic representation of call hierarchies, flowchart and structure diagram representation, Check MISRA rules, and determine a variety of metrics. This also includes cyclomatic complexity.

Klocwork is a powerful static analysis tool that supports C, C ++, Java, and C #. It can also check coding guidelines such as MISRA, HIS, Autosar C ++ 14 and CERT, and indicates possible errors at execution time, such as NULL pointer dereferencing or access outside of array boundaries. Also, it can determine more than 100 metrics, including cyclomatic complexity. CCCC stands for "C and C ++ Code Counter" and originated from a research project.

It is freely available through sourceforge.net. Java and C # supported. It can also check coding guidelines such as MISRA, HIS, Autosar C ++ 14 and CERT, and indicates possible errors at execution time, such as NULL pointer dereferencing or access outside of array boundaries. Also, it is able to determine more than 100 metrics, including the cyclomatic complexity.

The tools mentioned for the four code examples measure differently. For example, TESSY and DAC determine the value 5 for the cyclomatic complexity for the function func2 (), while Klocwork measures the value 2. This can be explained by the fact that TESSY and DAC increase the cyclomatic complexity by one for each of the logical operators in func2 (). So the value corresponds more to the "felt" complexity. The value 5 can also be justified by the fact that, for example, IF (a AND b) THEN can be formulated as IF (a) THEN IF (b) THEN. The value 2 measured by Klocwork is the value of "pure teaching."

Another discrepancy arises for the function f_switch () between TESSY and Klocwork, on the one hand, both of which measure the value 13 and DAC on the other hand, where only the value 12 is determined. For the first three functions, CCCC does not measure a value that is the same as the value of one of the three other tools. The CCCC documentation states that CCCC tries to provide a pragmatic approximation by counting language elements.

But even if you know the rules, you cannot always understand how CCCC determined the measured values. The CCCC values should, therefore, be treated with caution. Overall, the discussion above is not about what the correct value is, but that values provided by different tools may differ. All four tools determine the same value 2 only for the sine () function. sinus () has only one binary decision. Unfortunately, this value does not correspond to the perceived complexity of the function.

When introducing the cyclomatic complexity for the Fortran programming language in 1976, the inventor Thomas J. McCabe recommended that no software unit should have a value greater than 10. Otherwise, it should be split. McCabe describes the value 10 as a reasonable, but not magical, upper limit, not imposed by higher powers.

Which Cyclomatic Complexity Values Should You Aim For?

A division of the C function f_switch () from the picture above, which has a cyclomatic complexity of more than 10, is not sensible. Therefore, as with any other metric, it is advisable to collect comparison data in order to thereby tracking outliers. If, for example, in a project with 100 functions all have cyclomatic complexity with values less than 20, but two functions have values greater than 50, it is worth taking a look at these outliers.

However, if it turns out that it is due to extensive, but clearly structured switch statements, this can be accepted. You can also use other projects: If an earlier, comparable project with good software quality had low values for the CC, but the current project did not, so it can be a good idea to reduce the cyclomatic complexity in the current project.

McCabe also found that CC can vary from programmer to programmer. You also have to keep in mind that different tools obviously calculate cyclomatic complexity differently. In principle, some tools give higher values than others. Therefore the fixation on the ominous value 10 is questionable.

Chapter 6

Active Documentation

If at one end some define the problem to be solved and at the other end those who solve it, how can we be sure that we are all trying to solve the same problem? And, if we accept that the definition will need to be enriched, corrected, nuanced, and even that the problem to be solved will change radically during the life of the project, how do we maintain the same definition for all stakeholders, and more importantly, how do we ensure that our program solves the problem?

Functional Tests

To have some confidence that the application solves a certain problem, functional tests are carried out; these solve a concrete and representative example by simulating the user's actions and verifying that the application's reaction is as expected.

Functional testing must be kept up to date and evolve with changes in the application and its requirements. Another challenge is to make sure that they are correct, that is, that the behavior they are checking is really the one required for the application.

Functional tests must be automated; typically, they are written in the same programming language as the application. This allows us to execute a large number of them systematically and after each change, thus also protecting us from something that was working from stopping, that is, from possible regressions.

neverread

Let's say we have a customer who lacks time to read articles from the Internet.

- So many interesting articles, I don't have time to read them, but I can't ignore them either. I'd like to have an application where I can copy the address of the article I'm interested in.

- Ah, you want an application that allows you to store links to articles? The application would maintain a list of stored articles, which you could then access when you have time and read the articles.

- No, no, if I want the links to articles to disappear, if I had time to read them later, I would use Instapaper, man. It would be nice if I had a list of articles to read that was always empty; it would give me a great feeling of having everything under control.

- Er... -Okay.

From the conversation, we managed to extract an acceptance criterion:

- No matter how much we add articles, they will not be added to a list of articles to be read.

- The corresponding functional test will verify that the application meets the criterion for a particular example:

- When we add the article article/interesting.html, the list of articles to be read remains empty.

Functional tests, although not necessarily, are often conducted as end-to-end tests ([goos] p. 10), i.e., tests in which the application is exercised as a whole and from the outside, simulating the actions of the user and the collaborating systems, and evaluating the correction as perceived by the user and collaborators.

We have decided to solve the proposed problem with a web application, neverread. We will implement in Java an end-to-end functional test that verifies the acceptance criteria with a junit test that will start the application and then exercise and evaluate it. To simulate the interaction of a user through a web browser, we will use Selenium/WebDrive- r/HtmlUnit:

```java
public class ListStaysEmptyTest {
    private WebDriver webDriver;
    private NeverReadServer neverread;

    @Test
    public void articleListStaysEmptyWhenAddingNewArticle() {
        webDriver.findElement(By.name("url")).sendKeys("interesting/article.html", Keys.
        ENTER);
        assertThat(webDriver.findElements(By.cssSelector("li")).size(),
    }

    @Before
    public void setUp() throws Exception {
        neverread = new NeverReadServer();
        neverread.start(8081);

        WebDriver driver = new HtmlUnitDriver();
        driver.get("http://localhost:8081");
        webDriver = driver;
    }

    After
    public void tearDown() throws Exception {
        webDriver.close();
        neverread.stop();
    }
}
```

End-to-End Testing in Java (purejava/ListStaysEmptyTest.java)

Active Documentation

Although we could consider our functional test in Java as the main documentation where the acceptance criteria are recorded, depending on who is going to use it, this may or may not be an option. In addition, getting the readability of a paragraph in other than English replaced with a test in the programming language is a challenge, particularly if the programming language is as neat as Java.

Consequently, in most projects, it is necessary to document the requirements in a more textual manner.

One way to try to get the best of both alternatives is to connect the documentation to the application so that at all times, it is automatic and evident to verify compliance with each of the requirements expressed, which will help us to keep the documentation synchronized with the application and the client.

The documentation, together with the ability to process it for verification, will thus serve as a battery of functional tests; if we run this battery frequently (ideally with every change) and keep it accurate, we will be ensuring the proper functioning of the application for the specified definition.

Concordion

Concordion is one of the tools that can help us connect the documentation to the application; in Concordion, the criteria are written in HTML to which some marks are added that begin with concordion:

```
< p>
  When an article is added, the list of unread articles stays empty
</p>

< div class="example">
< h3>Example</h3>

< p>
  When the article
  <b concordion:set="#url">interesting/article.html</b>
  is added, the list of unread articles stays
  <b concordion:assertEquals="articleListAfterAdding(#url)">empty</b>
</p>
</div>
```

First test using Concordion (concordion/v1/ListStaysEmpty.html)

We see that we have expressed an example in the form of a condition and consequence that must be verified. The concordion:set and concordion:assertEquals attributes connect the document to the method of the backup class, written in Java, String articleListAfterAdding(String URL), which will do what the text says.

```java
public class ListStaysEmptyTest extends ConcordionTestCase {
    private WebDriver webDriver;
    private NeverReadServer neverread;

    SuppressWarnings(value = "unused")
    public String articleListAfterAdding(String url) throws InterruptedException {
        webDriver.findElement(By.name("url")).sendKeys(url, Keys.ENTER);
        List<WebElement> pendingArticles = webDriver.findElements(By.cssSelector("li"));

        return convertListOfArticlesToString(pendingArticles);
    }

    private static String convertListOfArticlesToString(List<WebElement> pendingArticles) {
        if (pendingArticles.isEmpty()) return "empty";
        else {
            StringBuilder stringBuilder = new StringBuilder();
            stringBuilder.append(pendingArticles.get(0).getText());

            for (int i = 1; i < pendingArticles.size(); i++)
                stringBuilder.append(", ").append(pendingArticles.get(i).getText());

            return stringBuilder.toString();
        }
    }
}
```

Concordion Test Backup Class (purejava/ListStaysEmptyTest.java)

When you run ListaPermanceVaciaTest, Concordion will generate an HTML document with the above text indicating whether the assertion is met by highlighting it in green or red.

Step By Step

Let's see what's going on here. We have written the acceptance criteria in ListPermaneceEmpty.html. In addition to HTML, we have written a class in Java that extends a Concordion infrastructure class: class ListPermaneceEmptyTest extends ConcordionTestCase.

When we run ListPermanennceEmptyTest:

1. Concordion processes the HTML.

2. Concordion detects the mark concordion:set="#url" and saves the content of that HTML mark (in this case,

3. "article/interesting.html") in the Concordion variable #url.

4. Concordion detects the concordion:assertEquals="articleListAfterAdding(#url)" mark, so it searches the accompanying class for a method called articleListAfterAdding and runs it, passing the contents of #url as a parameter.

5. The articleListAfterAdding method simulates the action of a user entering URL and getting the resulting list of articles.

6. Using convertListOfArticlesToString, we transform the list produced by WebDriver into a textual representation that can be compared with the text in the HTML. We have decided that the textual representation of an empty list will be "empty."

7. The articleListAfterAdding method returns, returning a string (in this case, "empty") that is compared to the content of the HTML markup in which concordion:assertEquals was found.

8. Concordion finishes processing the HTML document and generates another HTML in which the text that has the concordion:assertEquals mark is highlighted in green, to indicate that the assertion is fulfilled.

Maintaining the Appropriate Level of Abstraction

It is important to make an effort to describe the operation of the application in terms of the domain. For example, we could have been tempted to write the example as when the user enters a string in the text box and presses enter, the list of articles is empty.

However, that would be detrimental because it would take us away from the person who defines what the application should do and it would be more fragile, that is to say, as soon as we decided to change the implementation, for example, suppose that the addresses are entered by dragging them into an area of the application, we would have to rewrite the document.

As soon as the active documentation grows, the backup classes will need a significant amount of code. Some abstractions can help us reduce the repetition and fragility of the backup classes.

We can make the support class speak only in the language of the domain, for which we have to develop a dedicated language so that the method would look something like this:

```java
public String articleListAfterAdding(String article) throws InterruptedException {
    driver.addArticle(article);
    return convertListOfArticlesToString(driver.getListOfArticles());
}
```

Backup method using domain language
(concordion/v2_appdriver/ListStaysEmptyTest.java)

Another possibility is to abstract the web page in terms of the elements of the graphic environment, that is, to talk about visual elements of the page.

```java
public String articleListAfterAdding(String url) throws InterruptedException {
    page.enterIntoNewArticlesTextBox(url);
    List<String> pendingArticles = page.getArticlesInListOfArticles();

    return convertListOfArticlesToString(pendingArticles);
}
```

***Backup method using graphical environment language
(concordion/v3_pagedriver/ListaStaysEmptyTest.java)***

The abstraction layer in terms of the domain language is the purest option, but depending on the project, we may prefer a layer that is expressed in graphic terms or both, depending on the complexity of the project and how involved the client is in the graphic details.

Asynchronous Testing

In the previous sections, we have allowed ourselves a little cheating that we should discover before closing the article. Let's suppose that the developer, when writing the application code makes a mistake by not properly understanding what the client needs; he decides to make an application that adds the articles to a list of articles to be read. Our functional tests should detect this error by marking the assertion in red. However, we find that the tests pass.

Obviously, our functional tests are not correct, and this is because we are checking that the status of the item list is the same after entering the new item as it was before entering it, and the test verifies the condition before the application has time to add items to the list erroneously.

Trying asynchronous systems is complex enough to justify an article in itself, but if we list some of the options, from faster and easier to implement to less, we have

1. We tried only the synchronous part of the system. This makes testing easier and faster at the cost of reducing the range.

2. Introducing synchronization points. We'll be back to this one in a second.

3. We periodically check the assertion until it is fulfilled or the waiting time is over. In this option, it is crucial to adjust the duration; if we wait too long, the tests will take too long unnecessarily; if we wait too little, we will have false negatives.

In our example, we know that every time the application responds to the entry of a new article, the last thing it does is delete the text box. Therefore, we can use this event as a synchronization point; that is, before verifying that the list remains empty, we will wait until the box has been deleted.

```java
public void addArticle(String url) {
    webDriver.findElement(By.name("url")).sendKeys(url, Keys.ENTER);

    new WebDriverWait(webDriver, 2).until(new ExpectedCondition<Object>() {
        @Override
        public Object apply(WebDriver webDriver) {
            return "".equals(webDriver.findElement(By.name("url")).getAttribute("value"));
        }
    });
}

public List< String> getListOfArticles() {
    return webElementsToTheirTexts(webDriver.findElements(By.cssSelector("li")));
}
```

Synchronization point example
(concordion/v5_with_synchronisation/tools/NeverReadDriver.java)

Active documentation is a way of functionally testing a program in which each acceptance criterion is started with a text that links to the execution of code that verifies the criterion. When it is executed, a result is produced that indicates, in a way that is legible to domain experts, which acceptance criteria the program meets and which criteria it does not. Like almost everything else, its use should be adapted to the composition of the team and the complexity of the project.

Chapter 7

Seven Problems
When Testing Programs

Most computer professionals will agree that testing is one of the fundamental tasks of development, but if it is already difficult to learn programming techniques, much more difficult is to learn testing techniques, both manual and automatic. First, because, unfortunately, it is a piece of less widespread knowledge. Second, because it's even more abstract than programming.

That is why all the advice and shared experience we can draw on is particularly important. The following problems are focused on automatic testing, but many of them occur when doing manual testing as well. They are sorted by experience: the first problem appears mainly in teams that have never written tests, and the last one is even for developers with years of experience.

Like everything else, the proposed solutions must be applied with an understanding of why, how, and when they are applicable and useful, never if-guiding them blindly in all situations.

Save the Tests for Last

Although it is normal that as the end of each development cycle approaches, the testing effort (especially manual testing) is intensified, it is a major mistake not to have tested from the beginning of the development. This is not a cliché or a theoretical or academic consideration: not testing from the beginning of the development cycle has many disadvantages. For example:

1. The mental effort of testing a large program is much greater than the effort of testing a small program. You don't know where to start, it's hard to know when to finish, and it's easy to get the feeling that not everything is tested correctly. If we test the components that we create from the beginning, it is much easier to know how to attack the problem and do more complete tests.

2. If we test while writing code and know the quality level of the code, it will be easier to make estimates about the resources needed to finish the rest of the work. This will give us much more flexibility to renegotiate dates or features that will have to be left out, instead of going into a state of alarm when we realize, too late, that we don't have time to fix the bugs we find in the last few days.

3. When we have "finished" a project and all that remains is to try it out, it is normal to tend to "not want to see faults" or to play them down, to be flooded with a false optimism that confirms that we have really finished and there is nothing left to do. Especially if there are only a few days left until the delivery, and we feel that we cannot do much, and we

just want to deliver the result and forget about the project. This happens much less if we have professionals exclusively dedicated to testing, of course.

4. Testing from the beginning means that we will be testing for longer, so we will have found more cases that could be problematic, and therefore more failures (and the solutions to them) before it is too late.

5. All the tests we do soon will help increase the quality of the code, which not only affects the final quality of the product but also how easy it is to write and debug any other code that depends on the first one. Interaction failures between the two code bases will be easier to find, and in particular, the source of the errors.

6. If we write automatic tests from the beginning, we will force ourselves to write cleaner APIs. Generally, code that is easier to test is code that is more decoupled, cleaner, and more stable. Undoubtedly, one of the advantages of writing automated tests is that they help maintain a higher quality design. But if we don't try it from the beginning, we lose this advantage.

7. By not testing from the beginning, we will develop code that is not particularly easy to test, and then later, we start adapting the code to make it so, the more effort it will cost. Once we have written a large amount of code regardless of whether it is easy to test or not, the temptation to leave many parts untested will be irresistible. And, of course, if

we do not make an effort to adapt the code at that time, we will enter a vicious circle.

As sooner or later, the result of the work will have to be tested, and it is better to start early because it is less expensive (in time and mental effort), and the results are better. Writing untested code is simply irresponsible and disrespectful to the users of the product and the rest of the team members, especially those who have to maintain the code afterward and any team member who uses the untested code directly or indirectly.

Being too Specific in Checks

This is a fairly common problem, especially when you start testing. The automated tests are, in a way, a description of what the program is expected to do. A code specification, so to speak. As such, it should only describe behavior that we hope will not change. If we are too specific or demanding in our testing, our testing will not only prevent us from introducing errors in the code but also prevent us from making other changes.

For example, let's say we're writing a very simple to-do application. The class that represents a list of tasks is called BrownList, and it could look like this in Ruby:

```
class BrownList
  def initialize(db)
    # ...
  end

  def add_brown(title)
    # We insert in a database, return an id end

  def mark_brown_done(id)
    # We mark the id given as done end

  def pending_browns
    # We return a list of the tasks to be done end
end

# It's used like this
bl = BrownList.new(db_handle)
id = bl.add_brown("Pending task")
bl.mark_brown_done(id) list_pending_browns
```


of the implementation of the BrownList class

Now, to test that the add_brown method works, we may want to connect to the database and check that it has the correct row. In the vast majority of cases, this is a mistake. To understand why you have to realize that testing defines what it means for the code to work. Thus, if the tests use implementation details, it will be implicitly defined that the program only "works well" if it maintains the same implementation details. Which is, of course, a mistake, because it doesn't allow the code to evolve.

```ruby
class TestBrownList < Test::Unit::TestCase
  def setup
    # We recreated the test database to be empty end

  def test_add_brown_simple     MAL

    db_handle = ...
    bl = BrownList.new(db_handle)
    bl.add_brown("Test task")

    count = db_handle.execute("SELECT COUNT(*) FROM browns")
    assert_equal 1, count
  end
```

A bad example of testing the BrownList add_brown method

In this particular example, there are many cases where this test would fail, even though the code might be working perfectly:

- The name of the table where we save the tasks changes

- We added the multi-user feature, so there could be more tasks in that table than we want to count. We decided that we're going to use a non-SQL database, so the way to count would change

- We added an intermediate step of some kind so that the tasks would not be created initially in the database, but in something like Memcached, and a few seconds later they would go to the database

Testing should not limit us when we reorganize code or change implementation details. In fact, one of the advantages of having automatic tests is that when we reorganize code, we will know if we are doing something wrong because the tests will fail. If we are not sure that when a test fails, it is because there is a problem in the code, our tests are not helping us. At least, not as much as they should.

What we want to check in the test is really whether there is a new task added. One way to test this is to use the pending_browns method. One might think that this is not a good idea because, if there is an error in add_brown and another in pending_browns that cancel each other out, the tests will pass anyway.

That's true, but in most cases, it doesn't matter, because, from the class user's point of view, the class behaves as it should. When we discover the bug, we can fix it not only without having to change the tests or the code that calls BrownList but without having been any change in the behavior of BrownList from the users' point of view.

```
class TestBrownList < Test::Unit::TestCase
  def setup
    # We recreated the test database to be empty end

  def test_add_brown_simple
    db_handle = ...
    bl = BrownList.new(db_handle)
    bl.add_brown("Test task")

    assert_equal 1, bl.pending_browns.length
  end
end
```

The best example of testing the BrownList add_brown method

To finish illustrating this tip, let's imagine now that we write a web interface for our to-do application. If we want to check that the web interface is working properly, one (bad) idea that may come to mind is to compare the HTML of the page with the HTML we expect. If we compare the full HTML (or a screenshot), our tests will be very, very fragile. For example, our tests will fail when we make any of these changes:

- Change the id of some element or the name of some CSS class

- Change a site item or exchange the position of two options in a menu Add a new option or extra information

- Correcting a spelling mistake or writing a text differently

If our tests compare the exact HTML output, we are implicitly defining our application not as a web application with certain characteristics, but as an application that generates certain HTML strings. Since the user does not care about the generated HTML, but about the application working, we can see that this approach is not the most appropriate one.

A much better way to test a web application is to look for the interesting parts. For example, check that the title of the new task appears in the page content right after it is created. Or check that it's no longer there after you delete it. Or check that, when you rename a task, the old title no longer appears, but the new one does.

However, doing these checks directly can be tedious and can add some fragility to our testing, so it's best to decouple the details of the generated HTML from the checks we want to do. One of the techniques for achieving this is known as PageObjects, but exploring PageObjects goes far beyond the scope of this article.

As a summary of this advice, we can say that the tests should not only fail when there is a problem but should also pass while there is none.

Do Not Run Them Frequently

The tests are not an addition to the code, and they are an integral part of it. Running them is also part of the normal development cycle. If we don't run them often, they're not going to be as effective. First, because when there are failures, it's likely to be more than one.

In that case, it will be more difficult to find the origin of these. Is it a single error that causes all the failures in the tests, one for each test? Second, because if we've made a lot of changes since the last time we ran the tests, we'll have more code to check for the problem.

Running the tests frequently (ideally, after every change we make) makes it very easy to find the cause of the error, because the only thing that may have caused the failures are the changes since we last ran them. If we run the tests before we commit our changes to version control and we see that one of the tests fails,   it's enough to run git diff (or svn diff or similar) to see what changes must have produced the problem.

In addition, the higher the frequency with which we run the tests, the more confident we are that the code is working properly. As far as possible, in the world of programming, it is better to avoid faith: we will work more calmly and with more confidence if we can demonstrate that the code works in the cases covered by the tests.

The last important point of this advice is to have a "neutral" machine that runs the automatic tests we have, every time someone sends a change to version control. The advantages are many:

- Even if someone forgets to run the tests before sending the changes, we are guaranteed that the tests will be run.

- If someone forgets to add a file to the version control, that file will not appear on the continuous integration machine so that the tests will fail, and we will realize the error.

- The test results on the continuous integration machine are more reliable because it has the same configuration as the production machines. For example, if a programmer writes a new test that depends on a new module or a configuration change that only exists on that programmer's machine, the test will pass on your machine but will fail in continuous integration. This bug will alert us to the problem before the project goes into production.

- Since we have the test results for every change that has been made and executed on the same machine, we can know what exact change produced the problem, which makes it much easier to fix it.

Not Controlling the Environment

Another fairly common problem is writing tests without controlling the environment in which they are run. Part of this (bad) habit comes from the belief that tests have to be adapted to different circumstances and be as robust as the programs we write. This is a misunderstanding.

Let's go back to the previous example of the To-Do application. When we wrote the evidence, the steps were not:

1. Get the number of current tasks, call it n

2. Adding a task

3. Check that the number of current tasks is n + 1

The steps were:

1. Leave the database in a known state (in this case, empty)

2. Adding a task

3. Check that the number of tasks is exactly 1

This difference is fundamental. One might think that the first test is better because "it works in more cases." However, this is a mistake for the following reasons:

- Writing robust code requires much more mental effort, especially as the possibilities grow. Since we don't need that robustness, we'd better put it aside.

- The tests will be less flexible because we will not be able to test what happens in specific cases (e.g., when there are exactly 20 tasks, when there are more than 100 tasks, etc.).

- If we don't control and remake the test execution environment, some tests will potentially depend on others. This means that the behavior of some tests can change the result of others. In the ideal case, which is the common case, the tests can be run one by one independently and have exactly the same result.

- They won't always give the same result, even when we execute them on their own. For example, let's say there's a bug in add_brown that only shows up when there are more than 20 tasks. In that case, if we never delete the database, our tests will fail when we've run them enough times. And if we leave them like that, and there's another bug that only shows up when there's no task, the tests will never tell us about the second bug.

If we want to test certain initial data cases, it is clearer and more reliable to test those cases expressly and separately. We will have the advantage that it will be clear from reading the evidence which cases we cover, and running the tests only once will make us sure that all the cases we are interested in work perfectly. As a general rule, any uncertainty or indeterminism about the execution or results of the tests that we can eliminate should be eliminated.

We can end this advice with a thought: tests are not better because they happen more often, but because they show that a greater number of interesting cases work exactly as we want them to.

Reusing Test Data

When we start writing tests, something we often need is initial or test data (in English, fixtures). If we don't have an easy way to create those databases for each test, we will be tempted to have only one initial set of data that we will use in all the tests of our project. Although, in some cases, it may be practical to share test data between some tests, this practice can bring an added problem.

As we write new tests, they will need more contrast data. If we add this data to our single initial data set, some of the old tests may start to fail (e.g., a test that counts the number of tasks in the system). If we rewrite the old test to pass with the new set of data, we will be making our tests more complex, and we also run the risk of failing to rewrite the old test. Not to mention that if we continue on this path, we may have to rewrite two tests next time. Or five. Or twenty.

This is all related, in a way, to the problem described in the previous section: thinking about the tests as we think about the rest of the code. In this case, I think that having more test data is better because it will look more like the real case in which the program will be executed. However, in most cases, this does not represent any advantage, but it does have at least one disadvantage: when some test fails, and we have to investigate why it will be more difficult to find the real problem, the more data there is. If we can write our tests with only one test object, or even none, then so much the better.

Not Facilitating the Testing Process

The section on running tests often already mentioned that tests are an integral part of the code. Although they don't work exactly the same way or have the same properties, they do have to be maintained with the same care and effort that we maintain the rest of the code.

This section emphasizes that we must do our best to facilitate the writing of evidence. These are not an annoying necessity to which we have to devote the least amount of time: as an integral part of our code, they deserve the same dedication as the rest. Thus, our test code must be readable, concise, and easy to write.

If it is difficult to write tests, whether in time, mental effort, or lines of code, we have a problem to solve, whether it is reorganizing code, writing convenience methods or using any other technique that helps us. Unfortunately, many developers think that it is normal that it is expensive to write tests and do nothing to improve the situation. Ultimately, this causes the team to write less, and worse quality, evidence.

Let's look at a concrete case. Let's say we want to test the web interface of our to-do application. One of the first tests we would write would ensure that creating a simple task works. A first implementation could look like this:

```python
class TestBrownListDashboard_______MAL(unittest.TestCase):

    def setUp(self):
        # We redo the database and create the browser in self.driver

    def testAddBrownSimple _______MAL(self):
        self.driver.get("/")
        self.driver.findElementById("username").send_keys("usuario")
        self.driver.findElementById("password").send_keys("contraseña")
        self.driver.findElementById("login").click()

        new_brown_title = "My title"
        self.driver.findElementById("new_brown").send_keys(new_brown_title)
        self.driver.findElementById("create_brown").click()
        title_tag = self.driver.findElementByTagName("task-1-title")
        self.assertEqual(title_tag.text, new_brown_title)
```

Hard to write functional test example

Although in isolation, this code is relatively easy to read and understand, it has several problems:

- It's not as compact as it could be

- It contains code that we know will be duplicated in other tests

- It doesn't contain abstractions, so when there are changes in the application (say, the id of "username" or "password" changes), we'll have to look for where we refer to them to update the code

- It is not written using the language of the application domain, but using the automation language of a browser, so it is more difficult to read and maintain

A much better alternative would be the following:

```
class TestBrownListDashboard(BrownFunctionalTestCase):

    def testAddBrownSimple(self): self.assertLogin("user",
        "password")

        new_brown_title = "My title"
        self.createBrown(new_brown_title)
        self.assertBrownExists(new_brown_title)
```

Example of a functional test that is easier to write

The improvements in the second version are the following:

- TestBrownListDashboard now inherits a new class, BrownFunctionalTestCase, which will be a base class for all our test classes. Here we will add all the common code to different tests of our application.

- Since we have a base class, we no longer need to write the setUp method because it already creates the database and initializes the test browser for us.

- To log in, we simply call a new assertLogin method. Not only is it much more compact and readable, but if the details of how we log in ever change, we can simply change the implementation of this method.

- Creating a new task is as easy as calling a new createBrown method, and checking that it has been created correctly is done by calling the assertBrownExists method. Depending on the case, we might even have created an assertCreateBrown method, but for now, it seems better to leave both operations separate.

As you can see, a simple reorganization of the code (of the same kind we would do with the main program code) can have a very big impact on the ease of maintenance of our tests.

The need to facilitate test writing extends to all tasks related to testing our code, not just maintaining the automated test code. Let's say we write a client-server program. If every time we find a problem we are not able to debug it, or make sure it is really fixed or not because we don't have an easy way to test the client or the server separately, we have a problem. One of the several possible solutions is to have a test client with which we can send the server any request we can think of, and a test server with which we can send the client any answer we can think of. Tools to easily capture client-server traffic can also save us a lot of time in the long run.

After all, we are talking about the quality of our work, not in an abstract or theoretical sense, but in the most pragmatic sense from the user's point of view. If we cannot check that our program behaves properly, we will have many bugs left to discover, and therefore to fix, which will reach the end-users.

Relying on Many External Services

The last piece of advice is the most advanced, and it is the advice you should be most careful about applying. The natural tendency when creating test environments is to replicate something as close as possible to the real environment, using the same databases, the same servers, and the same configuration. While this makes sense and is necessary for acceptance tests and integration tests 1, it can be quite counterproductive in the unit and similar tests, where we only want to test relatively small components.

Relying on external services such as a database, a web server, a job queue, etc. makes testing more fragile, because it increases the chances of failure due to misconfiguration, rather than because we have found a problem in the code. As in most types of tests, such as unitary tests, we only want to test that a certain component works properly, we don't need to integrate it with the rest of the components. In many cases, we can replace those components with "sticky" versions that behave as we need to for each test.

A clear example of the advantages of using "sticky" components is the development and testing of an application that uses an API, both in the case that we write only the client and in the case that we write both the client and the server. Although we should use the actual server for integration testing, most tests will have a more limited scope (either unit tests or functional tests that only cover client behavior). For these we know, by having the documentation of that API:

1. What calls our application should generate in certain situations.

2. How our application has to react to certain server responses

Armed with this knowledge, we can design tests that are not dependent on the server. Not depending on the server has several advantages, among others:

- The tests run faster.

- Tests can be run without an internet connection or access to the server (including the server being running properly).

- When there are bugs, they are easier to debug and correct.

- We can try many situations that we cannot easily reproduce in a real server, such as not being able to connect to the server, the server returning any kind of error, returning certain combinations of data that are difficult to obtain, race conditions, etc.

It's not all the advantages, of course. If the server makes changes that break compatibility with the documentation we have, those bugs won't be discovered until the integration tests. Similarly, if our tests depend on a particular behavior, documented or not, and this behavior changes, again, we will not detect these failures until the integration tests.

Let's look at a more concrete example. Let's say we write a program that uses the public API of Kiva, an organization that allows, through microcredit, to lend money to people in need. Our application will show the latest loans listed on the Kiva website (say, 50), the information we obtain using the /loans/newest call. However, several cases are very difficult to prove with a real server:

- That API functionality only returns 20 items per call, so we have to make several calls to get all the loans we want.

- If new loans are added while we are making calls for 50 loans, we will have repeat loans, which we want to avoid.

- It may be that there are not 50 loans at any given time, so we will have to make do with whatever data there is (instead of, for example, entering an infinite loop).

- The server may have a problem and not return a correct response, or there may simply be connectivity problems between the client and the server. At the very least, we want to make sure, as in the previous case, that the customer does not remain in an infinite loop, making blind requests until we have received 50 loans.

Testing all those cases by hand with the actual Kiva server is virtually impossible, mainly because we can't get the server to return the answers needed to replicate each case. If all our tests depend on the server, we can't be sure if the code works well. However, all these cases are very easy to prove if we avoid connecting to the real server. The above cases could be written in JavaScript, using Jasmine, as follows:

```javascript
it("should correctly get items from several pages", function() {
  var fakeServer = new FakeServer(fixtureWith100Loans);
  var kivaLoanLoader = new KivaLoanLoader(fakeServer);
  kivaLoanLoader.fetchLoans(50);
  expect(kivaLoanLoader.loans.length).toEqual(50);
  expect(kivaLoanLoader.loans[0].id).toEqual("loan1");
  expect(kivaLoanLoader.loans[50].id).toEqual("loan50");
});

it("should correctly skip items duplicated in different pages", function() {
  var fakeServer = new FakeServer(fixtureWith100LoansSomeRepeated);
  var kivaLoanLoader = new KivaLoanLoader(fakeServer);
  kivaLoanLoader.fetchLoans(25);
  expect(kivaLoanLoader.loans.length).toEqual(25);
  expect(kivaLoanLoader.loans[19].id).toEqual("loan20");
  // The following case will be loan20 repeated, if the code does not
  work well expect(kivaLoanLoader.loans[20].id).toEqual("loan21");
  expect(kivaLoanLoader.loans[24].id).toEqual("loan25");
});

it("should stop when there's no more data", function() {
  var fakeServer = new FakeServer(fixtureWith30Loans);
  var kivaLoanLoader = new KivaLoanLoader(fakeServer);
  // The next line will be an infinite loop if the code is not correct
  kivaLoanLoader.fetchLoans(40);
  expect(kivaLoanLoader.loans.length).toEqual(30);
  expect(kivaLoanLoader.loans[0].id).toEqual("loan1");
  expect(kivaLoanLoader.loans[29].id).toEqual("loan30");
});

it("should stop on server errors", function() {
  var fakeServer = new FakeServer(fixtureWithOnlyServerError);
  var kivaLoanLoader = new KivaLoanLoader(fakeServer);
  // The next line will be an infinite loop if the code is not correct
  kivaLoanLoader.fetchLoans(20);
  expect(kivaLoanLoader.loans.length).toEqual(0);
});
```

Example of how to test the Kiva API dummy client

Testing programs is an important task, but it is quite difficult to do properly. However, if we start testing from the beginning of the project, run them frequently and make sure they are easy to maintain, our chances of producing robust programs will be much higher:

Chapter 8

Quality In Software and The Continuous Integration

Quality In Software

"Quality" is a widely used word but a rather elusive concept, at least when it comes to finding reliable ways to improve it or simply to maintain it once we have reached an acceptable level. This section will explore what quality is and how to improve it in our projects.

Meaning

The first problem of quality is to define it. There are many definitions, but my favorite one in the context of software engineering is "fitness for use." One of the problems with the definition is that it is very vague, but, paradoxically, the very fact that it is so vague is what makes it useful. Quality is a very complex issue, so simplifying it, far from helping us to understand, will only give us the illusion that we understand it. And the illusion of understanding is very dangerous because it makes us resist real learning.

The second problem of quality is to get all stakeholders to share what they understand by quality. This shared understanding will help us focus on the important objectives, which are the needs of the project client. This does not mean that only the aspects mentioned by the client are important: often, clients take several properties for granted (efficiency, reliability, etc.), and our job is to make sure that these are met as much as the explicit requirements. That is, quality requires technical aspects such as fast code or simple design, but these must be subordinated to the needs and wishes of the customer, implicitly and explicitly.

How to Improve Quality

As stated in the previous section, it is impossible to give a "magic recipe" for improving quality. In fact, trying to improve quality simply by following a list of steps is almost certainly a path to failure. No matter what steps we follow, what we have heard from them or who recommended them: our only way to achieve a good level of quality is to use our experience and knowledge of the context to decide what will help us in each moment. We have to be aware of what we are doing and take control of our decisions.

However, guidelines can be given to improve quality. For example: to always keep the what, not the how, as the guide for everything we do; to maintain skepticism and question how we do things and why; to be prepared to change how we work and fight against "cult charge programming" 2; to not believe in technology as the center of what we do; to realize that the main thing is not to make nice or easy to understand code, but to solve problems 3; to not believe that problems have a single or better solution.

This does not mean that tools, techniques, and customs are not useful. Not at all. What it does mean is that they will help us according to which contexts, according to which projects, according to which teams and according to which clients, but never in all cases. The other chapters in this book describe some of these techniques and tools, which are very useful and every good professional should know and master, but one of the main messages of this chapter is that knowing and adapting to the context is important and that blindly applying any of these techniques or tools is a mistake.

To illustrate the ideas in this chapter, and as inspiration to help think outside the more academic canons, the following sections show several example situations along with suggestions for possible solutions. There can be no single or "correct" solution in these examples, among other reasons, because no literary description can give all the information needed to make a good decision.

Example 1: Processes

As a general rule, having processes and rules helps development teams work more efficiently. On the one hand, it makes it easier for us to focus on what we are doing and not on how 4.

However, processes and rules can become obsolete. For example, let's say one or two team members cause problems with continuous integration: they often make changes that cause the test battery to fail, and they have no discipline in writing tests. Given this situation, we decided that each change sent to the repository must contain some modifications to some test files. The measure works

144

more or less well, those team members start taking the tests more seriously, and so we increase the team's productivity with it.

Now, all rules have good parts and bad parts, like everything. This particular measure can be annoying when we want to fix a spelling error in a comment, update the documentation, or reformat the code (since our change would not modify any test files).

Therefore, if at any time, those team members leave or get to the point of writing good evidence and not needing the above measure, it may be time to eliminate this rule. To maintain and follow the rules simply because they have "always worked" is to fall into the temptation of following the "cult of office."

Example 2: Test Automation

One of the constants in the chapters in this book is the use of automatic testing. While this is certainly one of the best and most useful practices, it is also true that we often have to work with legacy code (i.e., without testing). In those cases, what do we do?

For example, let's say we join a team that doesn't have an automatic testing culture, and we're late with the next delivery. A particular part of the code is giving quite a few problems, and manual testing (the way the computer tests the code) is not finding enough bugs, or not soon enough.

Although automating testing is probably the best idea, in the long run, there is no rule that is exempt from exceptions. The critical parts of the project we work on may not be easy to test with automated testing reliably, and insisting on emphasizing these at all costs does not help the team in the context of this delivery. Perhaps the stress of being behind schedule makes the team "optimistic" when writing tests, and the tests give a false sense of security.

The decision-makers may not be convinced, and in the short term, it may not be worth spending time and energy to convince them. And we may have convinced the decision-makers, but the team is not convinced, and trying to force them to write tests will only lead to low morale and a very poor quality set of automated tests.

And if, for whatever reason, we conclude that trying to implement automatic testing for the next delivery is not a good idea, what can we do? One of the possibilities is to start by making the team more effective without radically changing their work philosophy. For example, we may find after analyzing the situation that this part of the program is more difficult to test manually because it does not give enough information.

Perhaps adding a "hidden" option that makes that part less opaque may be sufficient until the key date. Or improve communication between team members. Because, among other things, it is always good to respect the way a team works ("which has always worked"): it not only improves the relationships between its members but also helps to gain their respect and attention, which will be necessary later on to be able to implement big changes such as test-driven development or simply writing automated tests. And in the meantime, we can gradually teach the team how to automate the testing to move to a (possibly) more scalable model.

Example 3: Specifications

When you develop software, you usually have specifications. They can be formal (a document) or informal (the shared knowledge of the team). The specifications aim to be able to concentrate on the technical solution without having to continually ask the customers or the rest of the team about the approach to solving the problem. But, again, the specifications are only a tool, and meeting the specifications more closely does not have to guarantee a higher quality of the project once it is completed.

Let's say we're developing the software that drives an automatic car. One of the requirements of the car is that it stops at pedestrian crossings when it detects that a person is crossing. However, many people don't cross at pedestrian crossings, so the car would be much safer if it didn't rely on pedestrian crossings, but could detect for itself if there was something in front of it that it could run over. In other words, specifications are a very useful tool, but they are never the ultimate goal of software development.

People who write specifications make mistakes, project conditions change, etc. Always maintaining skepticism and a complete vision of our objectives and not getting carried away with "it's not my job,""I don't get paid for this," or "I just do what I'm told," is much more important than meeting the specification diligently. In other words, our job is not to write software that fits a textual description of a problem. It's making useful software and solving problems.

Example 4: Simple Design

An important part of quality is, of course, having maintainable code. Maintainable code is usually achieved with readable code and simple design. However, like many other things, these two aspects are just a tool to achieve quality: a readable code and a simple design make the code, on average, less error-prone, and these will be easier to detect and correct.

Now, what if at some point the needs of the project collide with our (for now) simple design? The answer is obvious: the customer's needs are the number one objective, and the rest has to be adapted to them. Trying to adapt to the customer's needs to the design of the application is, in most cases, a mistake.

If to solve the new problem, we make the design less linear or more complex, and we are not "making a mess because the client does not have clear ideas" or because "he does not know how the application works": we are helping to solve a real problem. If that involves making a "botched" code, that probably means we have to revise the design of our application. Not because we have done it wrong from the beginning, but because we have discovered new requirements, or refined the ones we had.

One conclusion we can draw is that quality is difficult to achieve and measure, and it takes experience and a lot of work to obtain it. But the most important conclusion is that it is impossible to improve the quality of an IT project by applying rules or methodologies. No matter how much experience or how much knowledge the person who formulated them has, no set of rules or methodologies can solve our problems if we apply them without understanding what we do and in what context they are useful.

Continuous Integration

Regardless of whether the development team follows a classic cascade methodology or some kind of agile methodology, there is a decisive moment that determines the success of the project. This moment is the deployment of the application in the customer's systems, what we know as a production system.

Usually, this is a very tense moment because it is very rare that everything works at first. Following a methodology, in which incremental development predominates, where functionalities are delivered little by little, slightly minimizes the impact, provided that at the end of each iteration, it has been deployed in the actual production system.

But generally, it is still an uncomfortable time, and errors often occur because the development machines have different configurations than the production machines, the performance is not as good because the production database has a much greater amount of information or any other detail that was not taken into account during development.

To solve this problem, a new "philosophy" or practice called continuous integration has emerged. This is a slightly different way of developing than usual and requires a series of good practices and the acceptance of these by the development team. It has to become a habit that is carried out automatically, almost without our noticing it.

Continuous Integration From the Developer's Point of View

The following description of a day's work, in a team doing continuous integration, will help to illustrate the process and to understand the elements needed to carry it out.

At the beginning of the day, it is normal to select the next most important task to be performed. Based on the planning meeting six and the daily meeting seven, there is always a list of prioritized tasks available to the development team, so it is very easy to know what to do next. We select the task we must work on and return to our desk.

The first step will be to update the source code we have with the newest version available in the central repository. Similarly, if this is the first time we're going to work on a project, we just have to download a clean copy from the code repository and start doing our job.

Throughout the day, we will implement the new functionality, which should be small enough to finish in a day's work and should include a series of tests to verify that it has the desired behavior. You can read more about the tests in other chapters of the book, right now we will not go into the subject because there are whole books about TDD and unitary tests.

When the functionality is finished, before uploading any changes to the repository, we will update the source code with the changes of our colleagues and make sure that the application continues to be built correctly and that the project tests are green, meaning that they all pass without any problem. If, on the other hand, an error appears, we will fix it immediately.

Never, under any circumstance, upload code to the repository without checking that the tests pass correctly, and the application can be built without incidents. In addition, it is advisable to access the application and quickly check that everything is still working properly, as unit tests are usually not 100% covered since certain infrastructure details are easier to test by hand.

Once we have done all the previous steps, we can save our changes in the central code repository, allowing the rest of the team to update and have them available in a matter of seconds.

Although the continuous integration process started from the moment we started working on the new functionality, the continuous integration server starts working when we upload our changes to the code repository. This system will download a new version of the source code with all the changes made (ours and our colleagues), run the tests, and after making the construction of the project, will deploy it in a "replica" of the production machine.

Everything is fully automated. The continuous integration server itself could pass some extra tests, such as static code analysis, coverage analysis, or any other detail that would be very tedious to go through in the development process because it requires too much time.

There could also have been a mistake. In that case, the continuous integration server would alert us with a message in its console or simply by sending an email, which is the most common option. In that case, we will have to inspect what the error was and solve it to upload a new corrected version. Since the error is generated within minutes and not days or months have passed, it is very easy to find out where the problem is.

Advantages of Continuous Integration

Experience shows that it reduces incredibly the number of errors in the final product. This is probably the biggest advantage it brings because a final product with few or even no errors is ultimately the goal we all want as developers.

But we must not forget the other great advantage of this practice, the transparency of the process. Since we all work using the same code repository and the information from the integration server is public, for the whole team and sometimes even for the client, the real status of the project is known precisely. You don't have to wait for months to find out how things are going, and follow-up meetings can be short and precise.

An added advantage is the possibility of having a demonstration server where you always have the latest version of the application. This way, customers can test the latest changes daily and provide feedback to the development team without having to wait months.

Requirements for Continuous Integration

We now have a more concrete vision of what continuous integration is, but we would do well to review what the indispensable elements for doing it properly are.

Code Repository

The code repository is the fundamental tool that allows the team to work in a synchronized yet simple way. Everyone works on their own part and can update the changes without other developers having to wait for them and vice versa.

Unfortunately, there are still many companies that do not yet possess such a tool. For those who don't use a code repository yet, there are a lot of quality free solutions available today, such as Subversion, Git, or Mercurial, to name a few. This is a fundamental piece, and it will be practically impossible to carry out continuous integration if it is not available.

These types of tools mark a before and after in the daily work of a software development team. But it is also the fundamental pivot of continuous integration, which is not possible without a code repository.

Automated Construction System

Many teams use complex development environments to implement and compile projects. This in itself is not bad, but we should be able to build the project on any machine without the need for such environments. Not all the machines on which we are going to install our project will have the development environment we work with; even in some cases, they may have relatively expensive licenses, so it would not be a viable option.

Many different building solutions are depending on the programming languages, in Java there is Ant or Maven, in Ruby there is Rake, just to mention a few. The condition is that it must be a very simple tool that can be executed in any machine and that manages to automate not only the compilation process but also the execution of the tests of our application and even the deployment in the application server if necessary.

Daily Commitments

Not all requirements are based on having a certain type of tool, and some are based on knowing how to use a certain tool. Once we have version control, we must remember that the storage of changes must be daily; ideally, a developer must even make several uploads to the code repository per day.

If we have a code repository, but each developer uploads his changes every two weeks, we are still in the same problem as before, the integration of the project is delayed during all that time, losing any option to get information immediately. Also, delaying the integration for so long creates more conflicts between the files edited by the developers. Because with each repository update, integration of the entire project is made, every minimal change that does not disrupt the project must be uploaded to make sure everything is still working correctly.

Unit Tests

We talked all the time about checking that the project is working properly, and at the same time, automating the whole process as best as possible. To be able to check that the project works automatically, we need unit tests (often even integration tests).

There are many different ways to include tests in the project, personally, I think TDD is the most appropriate way, but if the team is not experienced and creates the tests after the implementation is done it is not an invalid method either. The fundamental premise is that any new functionality must have a battery of tests to verify that its behavior is correct.

Integration Server

This is the most controversial piece, and many people believe that it is not absolutely necessary to make continuous integration correct - for example, some teams do the integration manually with every upload to the code repository. In my opinion, it is such a simple and cheap step to automate that it is not worth saving.

Setting up an integration server, such as Jenkins or Cruise Control, is free and as simple as deploying a file on a server. On the other hand, the advantages are great. To begin with, the process is fully automated, which avoids human error. And on the other hand, it reduces the amount of work, as we have a prefabricated solution without having to create complex home-made solutions ourselves.

One Step Further

With the steps described so far, we would have a fairly complete process, and that will certainly improve the quality of our product. But we can go a little further and use the integration server to do certain relatively complex tasks for us.

For example, we could configure the server to do static code analysis, so that it can search all of the code for suspicious blocks, duplicate blocks, or unused references, among other things. There are many options, such as FindBugs or PDM. At first sight, it may seem irrelevant, but we must remember that complexity is what slows down the development process, so code with fewer lines and useless references will be easier to read and understand.

We could also include tasks that allow us to deploy the application on a server so that we would always have a demonstration service with the latest version of our project. This is really useful when we have a committed client, willing to test all the new changes and give information to the team.

Another operation that we can automate, and that the integration server could do for us is to perform system tests on the application. Let's imagine we are developing a web application, and we could create tests with some navigation recording tools, such as Selenium, and launch them with every construction the server makes. This is a very time-consuming type of test, and it would not be feasible to launch them with every developer's build, but for the integration server, there would be no problem. This is just one more example of how much a continuous integration server can do for us, and it will help us to keep a stable and tested product fully automatic.

To finish, I would like to use some comments heard by Martin Fowler when he talks about continuous integration with other developers. The first reaction is usually something like "that can't work (here)" or "doing that won't change things much," but many teams realize that it is easier to implement than it seems and after a while, their reaction changes to "how can you live without that?

Now it's your choice whether you decide to try it or not, but before you do, think about how little you have to lose and how much you can gain

Chapter 9

Test-Driven Development

Test-driven development (or TDD) consists of writing the test that demonstrates a feature of the software before the feature itself; step by step, a battery of tests is built up with the code for exploitation, at the rate of:

> red - green - refactoring

Where in the red step we write a test that the software does not satisfy, in the green one, we modify the exploitation code so that it satisfies it and in the one of refactoring we improve the code without changing functionality, with the confidence that the battery of tests that we have been creating up to the moment protects us of spoiling something without realizing it.

Example

Probably the easiest way to explain TDD is with a unit-level example. Suppose our application needs to convert miles to kilometers; we start with a test:

> *Red*

```scala
test("Converts miles into kilometers") {
    MilesToKilometersConverter.convert(1.0) should be(1.609)
}
```

First test (example0/MilesToKilometersConverterTest.scala)

Next, as we are using for the Scala examples, which is a compiled language before we can run the tests, we need to write some more code. We'll just add the minimum exploitation code needed for it to compile.

```scala
object MilesToKilometersConverter {
    def convert(miles: Double): Double =
      throw new RuntimeException("Not yet implemented")
}
```

Code needed for the first test to compile

To finish the red step, we run the test, checking that it fails (which many environments mark in red) by launching the exception we expected:

```
Not yet implemented
java.lang.RuntimeException: Not yet implemented
```

Although this step may seem trivial, it has forced us to make a few important decisions:

First, it has forced us to define the contract of use for the converter; in this case, the name suggests that it specifically converts miles to kilometers, and not vice versa; the conversion method is part of the MilesToKilometer sConverter object (and not of the class), so it is not necessary to create a converter object by calling new and suggests that it does not have state 9; miles are expressed as type Double; and so on.

Second and more fundamental, the test is an example that begins to define the functionality of the unit; that being expressed in a programming language protects us from the ambiguities of natural language. For example, we will not doubt the definition of a mile:

When we said miles, was it international miles (1,609km)? Nautical miles (1,852km)? Nordic miles (10km)?

The test has made it clear that the type of mile that matters in our application is equal to 1,609 kilometers.

Although it sometimes seems unnecessary, it is worthwhile, before progressing to the green step, to complete the red one by running a test that we know will fail; this forces us to think about the interface we are creating, and often reveals erroneous assumptions especially when it turns out that the test does not fail, or that it fails differently than we expected.

Green

The following is an increase in the operating code. The most purist thing is to write only the code that is essential to pass the test:

```
object MilesToKilometersConverter {
  def convert(miles: Double): Double = 1.609
}
```


And run the test, which our implementation will pass with green color if we use an environment that represents it that way.

Refactoring?

In this iteration, it's early to refactor. We move on to the next step.

Red

Before jumping to general implementation, it is worth considering other conditions of entry: do we accept negative distances? Since we do, in this case, we express it with another test.

```
test("Converts negative miles into kilometers") {
  MilesToKilometersConverter.convert(-2.0) should be(-3.218)
}
```

Second test (example0/MilesToKilometersConverterTest.scala)

We run the tests to see how the new failure.

```
1.609 was not equal to -3.218
org.scalatest.TestFailedException: 1.609 was not equal to -3.218
```

For readers more familiar with Java than with Scala, the objects created with objects in Scala are similar to the static part of the classes in Java; the methods defined under object are not linked to any instance of the MilesToKilometersConverter class - which in fact does not exist here. The truth is that these objects can have stated (in the same way that we can have static fields in Java), but many computers choose not to use this feature of the language unless there is a good reason; that's why we say that defining the method convert in the object suggests that the converter has no state.

Green

Now that we have two examples of convert functionality, it's a good time to look for a more general implementation ten that not only satisfies these two tests but also provides us with the general functionality that they exemplify. Like the one below:

```scala
object MilesToKilometersConverter {
    def convert(miles: Double): Double = miles * 1.609
}
```

Code for the second test (example0/MilesToKilometersConverter.scala)

We could have gone to the overall solution directly, and we will often do exactly that, however, as we saw in the previous green step, starting with the simplest solution and leaving the generalization for the next cycle, helps us focus first on defining what functionality we are going to add and what the contract of the unit we are testing is going to be, resolving ambiguities and uncovering erroneous assumptions. This will be particularly useful when we are not clear about what we want to do and how we want to implement it.

Refactoring

After every green step, we must consider improving the code, confident that the tests will protect us from breaking something that worked before. Refactorings can focus on detail (is it better to express thousands * 1,609 or 1,609 * thousands? should the parameter be called thousands or distanceInMiles?), but it is critical that we also often reconsider the design of the application and transform it into what is most appropriate for the current state of the code, without ignoring the future direction we want to go in, but without overdoing what we may never need.

Why and What For

The most important reason 11 for test-driven development is the emphasis on the function of our code and its suitability for testing and therefore use. This emphasis forces us to ask ourselves every time we are going to add exploit code: is this what I need, does it need to be done now, helping us to write only what we need and to keep the size and complexity of the code to the minimum necessary.

While TDD does not exempt us from deliberately seeking and directing the design, writing code that, from the first moment, is easy to test favors a certain simplicity and definitely evidences the coupling, guiding us towards the care of the collaboration between the units. In particular, the injection of dependencies and the separation between their interfaces and implementations, emerge naturally, since they facilitate automated testing.

Projects that are developed under test management have at all times a battery of tests per day, which documents the intention of each unit of the software, or combinations of units and the software as a whole. In addition, testing, while not guaranteed, gives a good indication of the correctness of the software, reducing the fear of breaking something and replacing it with a diligent habit of frequently refactoring and progressively improving the design.

Example of how testing guides us with respect to cohesion and coupling

In the following class, the translate method translates a text from Spanish to a kind of English, showing the result on the screen; this code is unlikely to have been developed guided by tests, since the main result, the translation, is not made available to the external code in any way that is easy to include in a test, but is manifested by calling the println method that gives access to the console, that is, through a side effect, making it difficult to verify from a test.

```scala
class SpanishIntoEnglishTranslator {
  def translate(spanish: String) {
    println(spanish.split(' ').map(_ match {
      case "yo" => "I"
      case "soy" => "am"
      case _ => "mmmeh"
    }).mkString(" "))
  }
}
```

Hard code to test (example1coupled/SpanishIntoEnglishTranslator.scala)

If we develop it with the testing facility in mind from the beginning, we will probably find that, to test the translation result, we need the code that translates to return the result; in fact, isn't the translation itself the main responsibility of this class, and not the display? If we could get the result, a test from our translator might go something like this:

```scala
var translator: SpanishIntoEnglishTranslator = _

before {
  translator = new SpanishIntoEnglishTranslator()
}

test("translates what it can") {
  translator.translate("yo soy") should be ("I am")
}

test("mmmehs what it can't") {
  translator.translate("dame argo") should be ("mmmeh mmmeh")
}
```

First test for the translator

(example2/SpanishIntoEnglishTranslatorTest.scala)

Which would lead to a translator less attached to the screen sample:

```scala
class SpanishIntoEnglishTranslator {
  def translate(spanish: String): String =
    spanish.split(' ').map(_ match {
      case "yo" => "I"
      case "soy" => "am"
      case _ => "mmmeh"
    }).mkString(" ")
}
```

An easier to test translator (example2/SpanishIntoEnglishTranslator.scala)

Test the Whole Application

So far we have focused on unit testing; however, if we are consistent with the principles we have seen guide us by keeping the focus on the objectives of the software, documenting and verifying-, we should consider it fundamental to guide the development of each part of the functionality using a test that exercises it as a whole; ideally, all functional tests should verify the whole of the software, in an environment similar to the operating environment, or even in the operating environment itself.

In practice there are often many obstacles, for example, it may be too costly actually to carry out certain destructive actions, there may not be enough resources or architectural decisions may have been imposed that make testing difficult; however, that does not mean that we have to give up completely; we will often achieve the most important improvements in the software and in the organization in which it is created by questioning the limitations.

Example

Let's go back to the initial example of distance conversion, and suppose we need to offer our customers a unit conversion service through a web service because we have decided that there are not enough converters on the Internet. The first test we are going to write, even before the ones we saw in the introduction is a test that exercises the whole application.

We will concentrate on a certain minimum increase in functionality, visible to the users of the system, that requires a reduced implementation and that has a high value from a commercial point of view or from the ultimate objectives of the project. In our case, we start with the conversion from miles to kilometers.

```scala
class ConversionTest
    extends FunSuite with ShouldMatchers with BeforeAndAfter {

  test("Converts miles into kilometers") {
    get("http://localhost:8080/1.0") should be("1.609")
  }

  def get(url: String): String = {
    Request.Get(url).execute().returnContent().asString()
  }

  var converter: Server = _

  before {
    converter = Converter.start(8080)
  }

  after {
    converter.stop()
  }
}
```

Functional test for the mileage converter

(step1/functional/ConversionTest.scala)

The get method is here a helper method for testing, which makes a get HTTP request and returns in the content of the message body. Obviously, getting this up and running requires some work, but if we concentrate on the basics, it won't be so much, and it will also help us to ask important questions about the system, particularly at the application level, for example: how will we communicate with the system; and about how we will test it. So, from the very first moment, the test facility is a full user of our project.

With this test as a guide, we will now concentrate ongoing through the entire system, almost at full speed, until we are satisfied. In the world of Java/Scala, the typical way to solve this is with a Servlet. Again we start with a test, this time at the unit level.

```scala
class ConverterTest extends FunSuite {
  test("Responds to get requests converting miles into kilometers") {
    val response = mock(classOf[HttpServletResponse])
    val printWriter = mock(classOf[PrintWriter])
    when(response.getWriter).thenReturn(printWriter)

    new Converter().doGet(mock(classOf[HttpServletRequest]), response)

    verify(printWriter).print("1.609")
  }
}
```

Unit test for the mileage converter (step1/ConverterTest.scala)

A more or less minimal converter using Jetty comes to be:

```scala
class Converter extends HttpServlet {
  override def doGet(req: HttpServletRequest, resp: HttpServletResponse) {
    resp.getWriter.print("1.609")
  }
}

object Converter {
  def main(args: Array[String]){
    start(8080)
  }

  def start(port: Int): Server = {
    val context = new ServletContextHandler()
    context.setContextPath("/")
    context.addServlet(new ServletHolder(new Converter()), "/*")

    val converter = new Server(port)
    converter.setHandler(context)

    converter.start()
    converter
  }
}
```

The first implementation of the mileage conversion service
(step1/Converter.scala)

As we see, the functionality we are offering is, as in the initial example, trivial. But reaching it has forced us to define the skeleton of our entire system, including exploitation and test code.

Next, we will progress, depending on our priorities. For example, we can concentrate on completing the functional conversion from miles to kilometers.

```scala
test("Converts negative miles into kilometers") {
  get("http://localhost:8080/-2.0") should be("-3.218")
}
```

Second functional test of the mileage converter
(step2/functional/ConversionTest.scala)

```scala
class Converter extends HttpServlet {
  override def doGet(req: HttpServletRequest, resp: HttpServletResponse) {
    val miles = req.getRequestURI.substring(1).toDouble
    resp.getWriter.print(miles * 1.609)
  }
}
```

**Code for the second functional test of the mileage converter
(step2/Converter.scala)**

The following is the handling of error cases, such as non-numeric
mileage amounts

```scala
test("Responds with 400 (Bad Request) and error message to unparseable amounts of miles") {
  statusCode("http://localhost:8080/blah") should be(400)
  get("http://localhost:8080/blah") should be("Miles incorrectly specified: /blah")
}
```

Test for mileage converter error (step3/functional/ConversionTest.scala)

```scala
class Converter extends HttpServlet {
  override def doGet(req: HttpServletRequest, resp: HttpServletResponse) {
    val milesAsString = req.getRequestURI.substring(1)
    try {
      val miles = milesAsString.toDouble
      resp.getWriter.print(miles * 1.609)
    }
    catch {
      case _: NumberFormatException => {
        resp.setStatus(HttpServletResponse.SC_BAD_REQUEST)
        resp.getWriter.print("Miles incorrectly specified: " + req.getRequestURI)
      }
    }
  }
}
```

Error Handling Code for Mileage Converter (step3/Converter.scala)

In addition to the red and green steps we have seen in the example
so far, as the application grows, we must both refactor at a unit
level and improve the design; for example, if in the next steps the
application needed to respond to different paths with different

conversions, we would probably decide to extract the analysis of the URIs to a separate unit and introduce different objects to delegate to depending on the type of conversion.

Testing One Thing at a Time

The maintenance of the test battery, which grows with the application, requires a constant investment of effort; having each test check only one aspect of the application will help us keep this effort manageable and also make them easier to understand, and therefore more efficient. Ideally, changing detail of the operation of our application should affect only one test that verifies only that detail, or, put another way:

- if it is relatively easy to change a certain aspect of the operation without any test failure, we have a gap in the battery coverage; 13

- if more than one fails, the battery has redundant code, increasing the cost of maintenance

- if the test that fails includes the verification of elements that are not directly related to our change, it is probably too complex, since introducing the change in the system requires taking into account aspects independent of the application.

Example of Focused Testing

Let's go back to where we left off with the example of the translator and suppose that the next thing we want to do is to separate the words from the original text not only by spaces but also by line changes. As we are guiding the changes with tests, we add to

SpanishIntoEnglishTranslatorTest, a test that verifies the new operation.

```
test("splits by change of line") {
    translator.translate("yo\nsoy") should be("I am")
}
```

Example of an off-center test

The problem with this is that the test mixes the separation of the original text and the translation of the words; the idea we want to convey with this example would be clearer if we could express the entry as "xxx\nxx" and the condition to be met as should be(Seq("xxx,""xx")); however, the current form of the system does not allow this, because the translation is part of the method we are testing.

Let's also suppose that the following functional increase would affect the translation of words itself, for example, by changing the source language to French or another variant of Spanish; this change would affect each of the tests in SpanishIntoEnglishTranslatorTest, but why should a test such as test("splits by change of line"), whose purpose is to test the separation in words, be affected?

We can see these deficiencies in our battery as the result of inappropriate granularity since the same test is checking several things: separation, translation, and word gathering. The solution would be to refactor before applying the change: perhaps the class that does the breaking down and composing should be different from the one that translates word for word?

We extract the word division to its own unit, so we can express, with a more focused test, the division of the text to be translated by line breaks:

```scala
class SplitterTest extends FunSuite with ShouldMatchers {
  test("splits by space") {
    Splitter("xxx xx") should be(Seq("xxx", "xx"))
  }

  test("splits by change of line") {
    Splitter("xxx\nxx") should be(Seq("xxx", "xx"))
  }
}
```

Word divisor test (example3/SplitterTest.scala)

```scala
object Splitter extends ((String) => Seq[String]) {
  def apply(s: String): Seq[String] = s split """[ \n]"""
}
```

Code for the word splitter (example3/Splitter.scala)

The translator receives it as an injected dependency through the builder.

```
class SpanishIntoEnglishTranslatorTest
    extends FunSuite with ShouldMatchers with BeforeAndAfter {

  var translator: SpanishIntoEnglishTranslator = _

  before {
    translator = new SpanishIntoEnglishTranslator(_ split ' ')
  }

  test("translates what it can") {
    translator.translate("yo soy") should be ("I am")
  }

  test("mmmehs what it can't") {
    translator.translate("dame argo") should be ("mmmeh mmmeh")
  }
}
```

Testing for a translator decoupled from the word divider

(example3/SpanishIntoEnglishTranslatorTest.scala)

```
class SpanishIntoEnglishTranslator(val splitter: (String) => Seq[String]) {
  def translate(spanish: String): String = {
    val split = splitter(spanish)
    split.map{_ match {
      case "yo" => "I"
      case "soy" => "am"
      case _ => "mmmeh"
    }}.mkString(" ")
  }
}
```

Translator code decoupled from word divider

(example3/SpanishIntoEnglishTranslator.scala)

The increased granularity has allowed us to ensure that the introduction of new functionality does not affect many tests. However, this has not been for free; we have increased the complexity of the code. In the end, all these decisions have to be evaluated one by one and decide what is most appropriate in each case, taking into account aspects such as complexity, execution time, and the direction in which we expect and want the project to go.

Keep the Battery Green

The test battery is the documentation of the functionality of our code. Documentation that is kept up to date, because it grows with each change and is exercised, i.e., we run the tests, at least with each submission of changes to the repository.

Working under test direction means always keeping the system working properly; ideally, the latest version in the common repository should be ready to be exploited at any time, and the tests satisfied at all times 15, so the documentation provided by the tests will always be up to date.

To achieve this, we must check the satisfaction of the tests before sending any change to the common repository; in addition, many computers are helped by a continuous integration system that automatically checks the battery every time a change is detected in the repository.

As the application grows, the time required for the full battery tends to increase, increasing the cost of development and motivating developers not always to satisfy the full battery or to space out change submissions to the common repository, both of which are very detrimental effects.

To keep test-driven programming viable, we must strive to keep this time short; the way to do this goes beyond an introductory section, but includes selecting and adjusting the technology used for the different elements of the battery, running in parallel, and even partitioning the application itself or making any adjustments that make it faster.16

Another problem related to the cost of the battery is intermittent failures, which will require a significant maintenance effort; we must invest the necessary effort to understand the root of each failure and solve it. Typical sources of intermittent failures are non-deterministic aspects of the software; for example, when what we are checking is asynchronous, we need to control the status of the application through synchronization points.

Some conditions are impossible to verify per se, such as the absence of behavior; in these cases, the solution is often to alter the application by revealing its state enough so that the tests can be synchronized with the application and know when the event we are verifying should have taken place.

Intermittent failures are also often caused by dependencies on elements outside the control of the test, such as the system clock, and the solution is usually to include and control this element from the test, for example, by altering the application's perception of time through a proxy that can be controlled from the test.

Reviews

Premature Design

The example of focused testing also illustrates one of the main criticisms against test-driven development: to test the kind of translation successfully, we have broken it down into a dictionary and a disassembler/word assembler; however, if we were really going to design an automated translation system this abstraction would not be appropriate, since the dictionary needs the context, the word arrangement in the resulting text depends on the grammatical function, etc.

Does this mean that the TDD has led us in the wrong direction?

As we said before, test-driven development means considering the tests as full users of our code, thus adding a cost in terms of the amount of code and complexity of the design that we choose to pay to benefit from the test guidance; opting for TDD is to consider this cost worthwhile. It would be less expensive to develop without the testing guide if we knew exactly what the requirements were and even what code to write from the beginning.

The TDD opposes this vision by considering development as a progressive process in which the team discovers what and how to develop, as it creates the application and gradually transforms, enriches and simplifies it, always moving from a system that works to another system that works, and that does perhaps a little more than the previous one.

Going back to the prematurity of the design, although it is true that the tests sometimes anticipate the need to decompose the code, these decisions become cheaper since the changes in the design are less expensive thanks to the protection that our battery gives us. And, in addition, this is also compensated by the countless occasions when we will not add complexity to the exploitation code because that complexity is not necessary to satisfy the tests, probably because it is not necessary at all for what we require from our application at that time.

Guidance through Functional Testing Only

Some experienced teams decide to use testing to guide development at the functional level, but not at the unit level, only writing unit tests when it is not practical to cover certain parts of the code with functional tests. They do this because they see unit testing more like a burden than as a useful guide in the internal design of the application, perhaps because they feel that their judgment is sufficient to achieve a good internal design.

Our recommendation is to start by guiding all units through testing and progress to a balance where we don't test at the unit level the obvious code, but where we recognize that code that is not worth testing because it is obvious is probably not very useful, and that code that is difficult to test is probably not useful at all. The recommendation is, in short, to apply common sense but not to give up the guidance provided by evidence in the development of the lower levels of the application.

Test-driven development helps us build applications where what motivates us to write the software guides every line of code, avoiding at every level to waste our efforts in developing functionality that is not exactly what we need, or that is simply unnecessary.

Test guidance, combined with continuous design, makes possible an organic development style, in which the team evolves the application, as it improves its knowledge of the domain requirements and the ideal implementation to solve them. In addition, the use of testing from the beginning reveals the coupling and encourages us to break the code into cohesive units with clearly identified dependencies.

While there is no absolute consensus on the suitability of test-driven development, many teams use it, particularly for commercial applications and in object-oriented languages. Our opinion is that, in addition to giving meaning and pace to each development activity, it makes it more fun, because it gives the developer more freedom to improve and enhance the software.:

Conclusion

Every programmer knows that you have to be pragmatic when it comes to carrying out your task; you don't have to waste time or resources in solving the problem that is on the table. The question comes in defining what it is to be pragmatic, since the term is, unfortunately, totally distorted.

According to Wikipedia, pragmatism is a current of thought that is based on the fact that only what works is true. This definition is very generic, and when we apply this concept to software, it is where the interpretations begin. If I had only worked with technology ten years ago, and I know it works, am I pragmatic?

NO. Pragmatism does not say that there is no need to renew, but quite the opposite. He says you have to use that technique that is proven with facts that work. This is where the lack of history in software development it can cause confusion, since there is no procedure to follow in which for problem A we have to apply solution B, and to complicate it further, new technologies and development processes that make old ones obsolete continuously appear.

Returning to the example of technology ten years ago And why not use that technology that works for me? Because as we said, I only know that technology. This means that I don't know if the rest provide better solutions to my problem, and I can't contrast if, with them, I could save development time, resources, or improve the user experience. In this case, at most, we can consider that we are practical, or worse, comfortable.

It is clear that the consideration of the pragmatic is influenced by the environment in which the software is developed depending on the time and resources available to make fudge can be considered to be pragmatic. Nothing could be further from the truth. Over time, all programmers see that the most costly stage in any project is maintenance. It is true that if the project has a high risk, the cost and development time should not be high for the investor. But that is no excuse to be professional when implementing the product.

In this and any other case, being pragmatic is putting all these variables on balance and finding the right way to carry the project forward. For example, we have a new idea that we want to implement as soon as possible. If we are really pragmatic, we will define what we want to do and start working on the product at the same time. Programming tools and methodologies that facilitate long-term change (design patterns, simple deployment, high-level libraries, testing, etc.) and some lightweight technology stack such as PHP, Node.js or Python would be used.

Apart from the needs of the market, motivation is key when it comes to avoiding what we could call being practical or getting things wrong, but soon. If a developer is not motivated, he won't mind making a fudge to finish the project for yesterday. And unfortunately, it will seem to him that he is pragmatic. What the one who has hired the developer does not know is that he is mortgaging his software and that it will be difficult to maintain that lack of professionalism, which will probably lead to a castle of unintelligible cards in the future.

So, is it possible to launch a project with low launch costs and low maintenance costs? Yes, you just have to be pragmatic, but really. And this probably can only be achieved with the experience, training, and collaboration of the client to identify what the needs are, laying the groundwork for the project to grow with the needs and challenges of the market.

The incorporation of requirements in the form of user stories and the involvement of those interested in the process will be crucial to keep the project alive. Here the use of design patterns (remember what is only true that works?), Which are nothing more than software design solutions tested in different areas, are of vital importance. To soak up good practices, there are also those considered as reference works, such as the Gang of Four pattern book, the book The Pragmatic Programmer or other works such as Clean Code offer knowledge of great professionals of the sector on which to build solid software pragmatically.

But this seems very complicated…

It may seem like a lot of work and very complicated, and in a way, it is. No one said that developing software was easy. Even so, as a first step, just asking yourself at work every day, what I am doing could do better, or better yet, could I avoid having to do this? They can exercise our pragmatic self and open our minds towards a better way to develop software.

With these first steps, it is easier to find the strength to document in references or learn new tools that allow us to get better and more maintainable products. And with this goal, to save costs and get better products, you have to be pragmatic.

References

https://dev.opera.com/blog/

https://www.martinfowler.com/

https://pypi.org/project/cache-em-all/

https://ruby-doc.com/docs/ProgrammingRuby/

https://en.wikipedia.org/wiki/The_Pragmatic_Programmer

https://martinfowler.com/articles/continuousIntegration.html

https://ec.europa.eu/research/participants/documents/downloadPubl
ic?documentIds=080166e5bb8be151&appId=PPGMS

https://gist.githubusercontent.com/mangelsnc/b94be87898cf73379e
ba93de7662125b/raw/48548b6ad1bdbf4cd9b357aa4577effa
4c861e17/Mailer.php

https://gist.github.com/mangelsnc/052fdb7c93dd57237fed7a9a449f
882c/raw/6fed7634ca98d76c7199114f6d0ca67abc2bb985/
Mailer.php

https://gist.githubusercontent.com/mangelsnc/0ee585fd6efeb90231f
38a3071b56d6e/raw/643e7ca72d0b07a12735fa61c4ea13a46
7938fb9/RegisterUserApplicationService.php

https://gist.githubusercontent.com/mangelsnc/d61e6e8f511875da4e
10fbd74bef8bea/raw/6d00f290d58d633ce9cdb5c328a3653c
7538ad4d/UserRepository.php

https://gist.githubusercontent.com/mangelsnc/1ae5819ac89c1c5474
ad4992167ebe33/raw/c1fb09df9e62c00657777ebaec5b8c00
3aca7d48/UserRepository.php